In the Grip of His Hand

No need to run or hide anymore. Let this Holy Spirit-inspired book bring healing in the midst of your pain, struggle, or desperation. You are loved right where you are. Let Ruth's story inspire you to affirm, for yourself, that you are "more than a conqueror through Christ" as you recognize you already have His victory working in you, no matter how you feel or what it looks like.

Arlene Bruinsma, RN, MSN,CNS, Christian therapist

Ruth has spent countless hours on her face before God and in searching the Scriptures through life's traumas, trials and tests. She has found the heart of God with a relentless passion in the pursuit of Who He is and what He says about her life's circumstances. She says in her book she is not a teacher, but a learner. I would say, through her desire to learn through life's experiences she has become a teacher, which reveals the depths of the heart of God and His Word, and which is conveyed throughout this book. From my own experience, she is an excellent teacher where the lessons of life have graced every lesson taught with richness only life's experiences can give.

The message conveyed to all through these pages is the great forgiveness and love of our Heavenly Father. How the Father yearns for all creation to know Him by having an intimate relationship with Him, that life's traumas and trials are not to destroy you, but can draw you into the arms of a loving Father, and bring peace in the midst of the storm. Ruth reveals to the reader how it is done, as she has walked through traumas many have not experienced, yet she has made it a lifestyle of running to Abba Father first. This book tells the reader how it can be done, as it is almost a mini-manual on living a life of being a lover of the King of Kings. *In the Grip of His Hand* is a book rich with Scripture that has brought life to all Ruth's experiences. The title is a description of Ruth's life in print.

Jan McIntyre, State of Idaho Director,
International Association of Healing Rooms Ministries

When I first met Ruth, I wondered where the depth of the richness of her walk with Christ grew from. Once I started reading her book, it became pretty obvious. Through trials and triumphs, Ruth describes how a dependency on Christ is the source of her strength—and tells the life story of how she learned it.

Steven Reames, Executive Director, Genesis World Mission

I have known Ruth and her testimony for the past decade. She is a woman of faith who lives what she writes. Ruth brings the presence of Jesus and the peace of His Kingdom wherever she goes. It is my great privilege to know her, and to call her my friend. *In the Grip of His Hand* is a powerful tool used in the Lord's hand to establish His rest in the hearts of those who read it. It is rich with purpose and the vibrancy of truth hewn from life's hardships and difficulties. Ruth has received precious encounters with God for the purpose of transform- ing her life, and by her testimony, transforming ours also. As you read this book you will be drawn into the Father's heart of compassion for you. You will learn anew how deeply He cares for you, and you will be reminded of your priceless worth in His eyes. I am so glad that Ruth revealed not only her victories, but also her struggles, that she reminded us that we can come to Him in our weakness and exchange it for His strength. May you be drawn into a deeper relationship with your Creator, and may you know Him as Ruth does, and call Him your Friend.

Carol Ruhter, minister, Break Forth Ministries

In the Grip of His Hand

In the **GRIP**

of

His Hand

Ruth Knoblock

SF

Simple Faith Books

Boise, Idaho

Published by Simple Faith Books
13347 W. Tapatio Drive
Boise, Idaho 83713

ISBN: 9780984236251

PRINTED IN THE UNITED STATES OF AMERICA

Dedication

*To my wonderful Lord Jesus Christ, the Savior and
Rescuer of my soul, my dearest Friend, and greatest
Comforter, whose Presence is my greatest joy.
My greatest reward in life is You.*

*And to my wonderful children, Russell, Kevin, Julie,
and Cindy, to my grandchildren and great-grandchildren
with my love, and the prayer that you will love Jesus with
all your hearts and walk with Him throughout your lives,
remembering that nothing can ever separate you from
His love.*

CONTENTS

Acknowledgments

I wish to express my thanks and appreciation to all those who supported this undertaking with your prayers, love, and words of encouragement. My special thanks to Alisa King for your dedication, creative talent, and the many hours you prayerfully invested to produce the beautiful cover. My special thanks and appreciation to my editor, Marilee Donivan, for your many hours of skillful and prayerful editing, your encouragement, and commitment to the completion of this book. This book could not have become a reality without your contributions.

Foreword

Ruth Knoblock has a true and abiding love for her Lord and Savior Jesus Christ and wishes to bring Him all the glory for being the Author and Creator of her life. God has blessed Ruth with a story, His story which she has been willing to write down and share with others.

In the Grip of His Hand will bless one's life with insight, encouragement, and Truth. Ruth's story is one of victory— victory over a fearful childhood, victory over a stagnant marriage, victory over the death of a beloved son, victory over depression; victory through Christ Jesus. Ruth's story, filled by the power of the Holy Spirit will arm you, shore you up, and give you the confidence and encouragement you need to live out the dream and vision God has for your life.

Ruth tells us, "There is that special something for which you were created and which He wants to fulfill through you on this earth. You have only to believe and ask. Only He can make a miracle out of impossibility. He does and He will!" Ruth strives to live her life for the Lord and she blesses others by doing so.

I truly believe that God brings people alongside us to walk His walk with us on this earth. God has brought Ruth into my life through her book, *In the Grip of His Hand*, and she has become a mentor, prayer partner and friend, even though we live states apart from each other. God answers our prayers in surprising ways sometimes (most of the time) if we just sit, be still, and take in every detail of what's going on around us. It is in the little things that we may find God in big ways. Ruth has most certainly helped me to make this discovery and I am forever grateful.

I can assure you that you will be blessed beyond belief by Ruth's story, *In the Grip of His Hand*. Let the blessings begin!

Sheri Woods, owner,
Jericho Coffee & Books

A Personal Message to Readers

"My heart is overflowing with a good theme; I recite my composition concerning the King; my tongue is the pen of a ready writer."

Psalm 45:1- NKJV

At the urging of others, this book is a labor of love and gratitude to my King, the Lord Jesus Christ. His passionate love pursued and rescued my soul for eternity and gave me purpose for living. That purpose is to declare His redeeming love, strength and power to this generation and to those who are to come.

God's heart and eyes search throughout the entire earth, looking for those whose hearts are open and responsive to His love, who will give their lives fully to Him. His heart longs for the lost, the abused, and abandoned, the outcasts, and the broken-hearted, with a love that can only be measured by Jesus' death on the cross. No words can describe or paint a true picture of His suffering for us. He laid down His life for us so we might be given life with Him in His kingdom for eternity. His sacrifice forever opened the door of access into the Father's heart to everyone who will believe that Jesus is the Son of God and receive Him into their hearts as personal Savior and Lord. He is the rescuer of human lives and this story is about one such rescue—my own. I am forever grateful, amazed, and humbled by His love for me and the price He paid to redeem me.

It is my hope you will be encouraged and comforted to know, regardless of your circumstances or the background from which you've come, that if your heart is open and longing to find God, He will make Himself known to you right where you are. He will hear the simplest prayer from a sincere heart if you will ask. He pursues you with His relentless love. No obstacle, your own weaknesses, doubts, or fears can keep Him from reaching for your hand and heart to bring you from darkness to light, death into life, and an eternal relationship with Himself.

May God use the message in these pages to reveal His grace, truth, and redeeming love through Jesus Christ. May His love touch and turn your heart toward Him Who is the rescuer, redeemer, and restorer of your soul. May your heart be gripped by the reality of His love for you and Who He is—your only source of hope and redemption, power, and purpose for living. He is the One Who saves, heals, delivers and restores. This is His story. To Him be the glory.

Ruth Knoblock

Chapter 1

Rescued

My early childhood was well acquainted with fear. I am so thankful that God sees beyond our fears, sins, and weaknesses to our potential and the person He created us to be. He sees the person we can become when we look to Him and give our life fully to Him and His purposes.

Children are of premium worth and value to the heart of God. That's why in Jesus' earthly ministry He rebuked the disciples for trying to keep the little children from coming to Him. It's a sobering thought that God has entrusted to parents the nurturing and care of their children, the responsibility of directing their hearts toward Him and teaching them His ways. All too often children have missed out on this crucial part of their development in life which has left them floundering and lost, without direction or sense of purpose. Thankfully, God's mercy and grace are greater than our failures. He is always ready to forgive and restore us, and even goes so far as to bring His redeeming love into that place of failure. Saving and restoring lives is His specialty.

My parents did not know the Lord, yet they taught us the principles of right and wrong, for which I am thankful. They loved and cared for us in the best way they knew. They were good parents in many ways, and later in life when I was in desperate need, their love was there to support and sustain me. I honor their memory and the good they taught us. I'm happy to say that many years later, both my mother and father came to know the Lord, and I was given the joy of leading my father to Christ when he was 68 years old.

Like any of us who are parents, even in doing our best, we all make mistakes. However, let me clarify that the poor and misguided choices I made as a teenager were my own, not theirs, and they were not responsible. I only share the following information to let you see the background which instilled my fears in childhood. It's interesting that even in the sharing of these memories, God has given me further understanding of why fear was such a huge part of my life from an early age.

My father was a practical joker who delighted in pulling pranks. He thought it was a laughing matter to see me scream and cry in fright. One such prank was during a camping trip where he and my mother had left my older brother, Lee, and myself at our campsite while they went to the store. I was five years old and Lee was ten. On the way, they decided it wasn't a good idea to leave us alone, so Dad had Mother drop him off with the the plan of going back to be with us. Of course, he didn't inform her of his intention to scare us. He circled back and came to our camp from the woods. Hiding behind a huge bush on hands and knees, he made vicious growling sounds, mimicking those of a wild animal.

Lee hid me under the picnic table from where I viewed the entire scenario. Terrified as I was, that was the only time in my life I didn't mind being in close proximity to a community of spiders! Lee went after him with a hunting knife in one hand and a hatchet in the other, shouting, "Are you human?" "If you're human, you better come out of there! Human or not human, here I come!" (He was always my protector.) When Lee threw a huge green pine cone at him, he came out from behind the bush laughing, thinking it was so funny. Lee was livid with anger, I was crying and shaking. Mom was highly upset and angry when she learned what Dad had done.

There were other situations, which I'll not elaborate on here, in which he played his jokes on us. One thing to be said from my experiences of being frightened, I learned you can run as fast as you have to! I used to have nightmares about running from someone and flying to get beyond reach of danger. In looking back, I can see why much of my growing up years conditioned me to fear.

We moved a few times during those early years, one of which took us to a small town in Oregon where we lived for four years. There I met a friend who invited me to attend church with her. She would walk to my house and from there each Sunday we walked to the nearby Community Bible Church. I loved the services, singing the songs about Jesus, and learning of Him.

One day, at the close of the service, as the pastor gave the invitation, his daughter put her arm around my shoulder and asked me if I would like to receive Jesus as my Savior. When I said yes, she led me to a small prayer room where we knelt in prayer and there I gave my heart to Him. I was ten years old at the time, and will never forget the deep sense of joy that came as I received Him that day. A memento I still have from that time is a small wooden plaque with a cross and the words "Jesus Saves" which I burned into it. My favorite memories of growing up are of the time spent in the church there and the meaningful activities we shared. They welcomed me with open arms and made me a part of the church family.

The Dream

Shortly before I gave my life to Christ, I had a very vivid dream one night as I was in a deep sleep. Every moment of it is etched in my memory as though it occurred last night.

The scenes before me were in clear color and very detailed. In the first, I was standing on the shore of a large body of water looking across the sea toward the distant shore. Standing on the opposite shore was Jesus, robed in brilliant white with a long golden sash crossed over His chest. Though it was a distance, I could clearly see His eyes were fixed on mine with an intense look of love which drew my heart. Without saying a word, He took a step toward me, leaned forward, and made a wide sweeping motion with His right arm as if to say, "Come on!" My heart leaped with joy and everything within me wanted to run to Him, but I looked at what was in front of me between us. My heart and feet froze in fear at the sight before me. Unable to speak, all I could do was cry.

With tears streaming down my cheeks, I could only shake my head, thinking, "No, I can't!"

What I saw in front of me was a sea of huge, stormy waves, shark-infested waters with dorsal fins exposed above the water. Without a word, Jesus came walking across the top of the water to me, gripped me by His right hand and walked me back across the top of the waves to the opposite shore. As we were walking over the waves, I could feel the mist on my face and a sense of exhilaration and joy as we walked hand in hand on the water. As we neared the shore, I awoke from the dream. When I opened my eyes, I was lying on my left side, my left hand still cupped and warm, feeling as if He still had me by the hand.

I never shared a word of the dream with anyone for many years for two reasons, the first being I didn't know what it meant at the time; secondly, that others wouldn't believe me. All I knew was Jesus was with me and had me by the hand. Only years later did I begin to understand its meaning and full significance as the events and seasons of my life unfolded into the reality of the dream. The stormy waves represent the crises, trials, and storms which come to all of us in life that threaten to overcome us. The sharks represent the assignments of the evil one designed to destroy us, and abort our destiny in Christ. I have watched it come true in circumstances time and again where my own weaknesses and fears would have brought me to certain defeat. In all the trials and where the enemy's assignments would have destroyed me, God arose in my behalf as the strong One and with His own right hand held me up, strengthened and rescued me. He is mighty to save!

Drifting Away -- Coming Home

After the wonderful experience of my new beginning with Christ there in Oregon and the joy I had in Him, our relationship suffered a setback when three years later we moved to Phoenix where there was no church within walking distance. Without Christian fellowship and the teachings from God's Word, I began drifting away from Him, not intentionally, but through neglect and ignorance of how to maintain my relationship with Him. Six months later in my sophomore year we moved to northern Arizona where I finished high school. The desire for church never left me, and occasionally friends would invite me to go with them, which I did gladly. Once in awhile I would attend the youth group, but most of our weekends were spent out of town.

Our home life was highly dysfunctional and unhappy, filled with alcoholism, bickering and strife. Like many young people without direction or encouragement and living in an unhealthy environment, I wanted out of there. I naïvely thought that marriage and a home of my own would bring the security and safety for which I longed. Motivated by fear and ignorance, I married shortly after graduation from high school. It was a tragic mistake which left me abandoned with a two-year old son and seven months pregnant with another. There had been the threat of physical violence and we were left for days without food, money for doctor visits or anything else.

The only Bible I had was a New Testament which had been given to me by the church years earlier. As I thumbed through the pages, my eyes fell on Jesus' words in Matthew 11.28-30 (NIV): *"Come to me, you who are weary and burdened, and I will give you rest. "* In desperation I walked outside, sat down on the porch, looked up at the stars, and broke down and wept. I asked the Lord's forgiveness for drifting away and not living for Him. At that moment I recommitted my life to Him with the promise that I would live for Him the rest of my days and raise my children to love and serve Him. I asked Him to help us and guide our path. Shortly after that I called my father and he came to get us and brought us home to California to live with them.

When my newborn son, Russell, was three weeks old, he developed an eye infection which put him in the hospital in CCU. He was critical, and we almost lost him. He was so tiny and helpless there in that huge bed that my heart broke for him. Again I cried out to God for his healing, and He heard my prayer. Rusty (as we called him) slowly recovered. The lack of money for doctor visits and vitamins during my pregnancy caused him to have serious health problems and my own recovery was slow, too. It was many months before he was well.

It took many more for me to recover physically, mentally, and emotionally to the place where I was able to look for a job. The doctor informed Mom that I was close to a nervous breakdown and advised her as to what she should do to help me recover. She began by giving me a list of a few things needed from the grocery store, insisting that I get out of the house and drive there. It forced me to interact with people again. It was such a simple thing and may seem ridiculous to some, but it was a difficult step forward for someone in my frame of mind. My parents were so good to us, and I thank God they were there. I don't know what might have happened to us without their love and support.

Out of that tragedy I was given several wonderful blessings. The first and most important was the restoration of my relationship with Jesus, and God's gift to me of two beautiful sons, David and Russell. My parents' love was also a huge blessing and gift to us.

When I was able, the first thing on my priority list was to take my boys to church. We began attending a small church where we were met with much love and acceptance. The pastor loved Jesus with a passion. Because of that, we grew in our love for the Lord. It was wonderful to see how the boys loved hearing the Bible stories and singing the songs about Jesus. It felt so very good to be back home in fellowship with God and His people again. We began to thrive.

When we turn to God in our desperate times with humility and repentance, He will always be there to bring forgiveness and the comfort of His presence. He does indeed work in all things for the good of those who love him.

This chapter would not be complete without sharing with you about the "good" that God brought to David, Russell, and me after our lives were torn apart. Though I deeply appreciated the home we had with my parents, a year and a half later I felt it was time to make our own way. They helped us move to Phoenix where I secured a job as a legal secretary. Through a mutual friend, Jim Knoblock came back into my life. He was an old friend from high school days whom I had previously dated. We began seeing each other, and about eight months later we were married. Shortly after our marriage, he adopted the boys as his own. He was God's provision for us and we were God's provision for him. Then, two years later, we were blessed with another wonderful son, Kevin, and later, a beautiful daughter, Julie. A few years later, Cindy came to be a part of our family through her friendship with Kevin and Julie.

I am so blessed to have such wonderful children who take care of me and show their love in so many ways. My children and grandchildren are a huge part of the "good" I've gained, which far outweighs any loss. God has blessed me with His best! This story is all about His faithfulness and the great things He has done!

Chapter 2

Beauty from Brokenness

In my hand is a small, beautiful aqua-blue stone, translucent and smooth, polished as though it came out of a tumbler. Indeed it did, for the sea had served as a tumbler in which a piece of ordinary broken glass was transformed into a beautiful stone. The process from which it emerged required years of being swept through the waters of the sea, buffeted by the currents, sharp edges removed by the swirling sand until it became smooth, polished, and beautiful.

It takes me back in memory to a small stretch of private beach along the Mendocino coast of California. It was October, 1982. I had remarried. My husband and I had taken a trip for a much-needed time of refreshing and rest after a devastating crisis in the church had left me broken in heart and soul. We stayed at a beautiful bed and breakfast inn overlooking the ocean with access to a private beach below. The next morning as we walked along the beach in the sunlight, my attention was drawn to some brightly-colored stones scattered along the water's edge, beautiful and shiny from the reflection of the water and sun. They were everywhere, like sparkling gems of various colors on a blanket of white sand.

My hands couldn't gather them fast enough, with the enthusiasm of a child finding a treasure. As I stood there gazing at them in my hands, the Lord spoke to my heart in a way which brought an awareness of His presence and the tender assurance of His love. His message to me was that the stones were once just pieces of broken glass with no beauty in them. They had been through the process in the sea of being buffeted, sanded, polished, and transformed into objects of beauty, now reflections of His handiwork. I was reminded of the verse in I Peter 2:5 (NKJV) which says: *"You also, as living stones, are being built up a spiritual house, acceptable to God through Jesus Christ."*

He said to me, "You are my living stone and beautiful to Me. I'm creating something beautiful from your brokenness which will reflect My glory." I stood there, the tears streaming down my face as I looked up to the heavens and said, "Thank You, Lord." It was a divine epiphany, an encounter with my Creator, which started my heart on its journey toward healing.

After our return home, I wanted to create something as a reminder of my encounter with God, a remembrance for years to come that could be shared with others. Using a beautiful piece of driftwood, a few of the stones and bits of moss, I fashioned a centerpiece which now decorates my bookcase as a beautiful reminder of the greatness, faithfulness, and love of my Creator and how He touched me.

The stones from the sea are a great analogy of the process God takes us through in life to transform us into the person we were created to be. It is the perfect picture of how He uses the broken places in our hearts and lives from which to bring His healing love to restore us. His desire is to shape and transform us until we reflect the beauty of His character to those around us. Just as the waters of the sea are always moving and never still, so in life there are ongoing changes, transitions which are forced upon us in the life-altering events and circumstances in which we find ourselves. Life-changing events which forever shape the person we become are as unpredictable as the storms and currents in the sea. Life never stays the same; people and relationships change. Just as the stones from the sea were shaped by the surrounding pressure of the elements and waters carrying them, we, too, are affected by the pressures in life which surround us.

However, unlike the stones which have no life or choice in what they become, we have been created in the image of our Creator. He gave us a free will to choose how we will respond to life's pressures and circumstances. We are honored as His highest creation in whom He invested His heart and deepest desires. We are, and will continue to be, faced with choices each day which will affect all of our tomorrows and our destiny. Our character determines our destiny, and our choices affect the lives of those around us.

We may not be able to choose or change the circumstances we find ourselves in. However, we do choose the way in which we will walk within them, and how we will respond with choices that can lead to life or death. We cannot afford to adopt a "victim" mentality in which we blame parents, siblings, spouses, society, or God, for our attitudes and choices.

The intentionality and passion of God's heart is that we would choose life and blessing in a relationship with Him which He offers through His Son, Jesus Christ. If we will choose Him, He will not only save and restore us from life's destructive forces, but will use the very circumstances of our past, as well as the present, to build a platform from which we can proclaim and demonstrate to the world around us the message of His redeeming love.

God's kingdom is built from broken things, beginning with Jesus and the sacrifice He made when He laid down His life for us on the cross. Truly His life was broken, spilled out and freely given from His heart of love to all who would come to Him in simple faith to receive the gift of eternal life with Him.

His blood bought our redemption and the forgiveness of our sins because of the riches of His grace. Everyone who believes in and receives Him as their Savior and Lord has been given the privilege of adoption into God's family as His son or daughter for eternity.

A great many souls down through the ages have come into God's kingdom, floating in the sea of humanity on the broken pieces of their lives. Those who have been fortunate enough to have come to a personal relationship with Jesus in a loving Christian home are truly blessed to have escaped the devastation of their childhood that so many have experienced. Fortunately, God's love is all-encompassing and knows no limits. There is nothing too hard for Him and with Him all things are possible. He came to redeem and restore broken lives.

Chapter 3

Encounters in the Redwoods

As we left the inn and our beach memories, we journeyed on to the Avenue of the Giants, a nineteen mile stretch of highway winding its way through the most beautiful redwoods I've ever seen. Majestic, ancient, centuries old, some of these monarchs have been here since before Christ walked the earth. To drive or walk through them is like stepping back in time to another world. Without the roar of the freeway or city noise, there is just quiet, shaded beauty with shafts of sunlight filtering through the trees. If you listen to the quiet, you can hear a bird calling here and there, and the echo of another in the distance.

As we wandered among them, a quietness came to our souls and a rest of spirit that left us in awe of our Creator. Our hearts were touched there in the silence and made aware of His presence. Having our picture taken in front of one of them made us acutely aware of how small we are in light of His vast and immeasurable creation. At one point I walked over to one named The Grandfather Tree, stretched out my arms and leaned against it, wanting to be close to this ancient living thing God created, its life spanning many centuries. For the first time in my life I became a tree hugger!

We proceeded on through the redwoods and came to one which was so huge in circumference a car could be driven through it. It was three-fourths dead, but out of the life remaining was a new tree growing 185 feet tall. I walked inside and looked around at the gutted shell of the old tree. It had been destroyed by fire and carved on by man. As I was standing there inside, it was as if God put His arms around me and I was prompted to look up. When I did, I could see through the hole in the top, out of which a new tree was growing. I felt God's presence and heard His message of love and assurance which brought further healing to my heart.

I clearly heard Him say, "No man, nor the enemy, nor anything can ever destroy the life I have created within you. Just as I am growing a new tree, I am growing a new you." I wept with thanksgiving and worshiped Him out of my pain.

We continued on for a few miles, then pulled over to walk among the trees again before having to leave the beauty and head for the freeway. As we walked along the path, we came to a special spot where some moss flowers were growing. We were so touched by God's greatness and the beauty of this place that we knelt down and prayed together. It was as though we were on holy ground. My husband made the comment that if God were to choose any spot on earth to dwell, he thought it would be there among His trees. It felt as though we were in a giant cathedral—and I believe we were, one not made by human hands.

It was an awesome and beautiful trip in which God revealed Himself and His love to me as my Creator, bringing a measure of much-needed healing to my heart. As a souvenir from the redwoods, I picked up a tiny pine cone to bring home as a reminder of His goodness and how He met me there. He knows the needs of His children and is so desirous of meeting us in the way we need. I am continually amazed by His love and personal care for each of His children. We are never out of His reach.

When I am out in the beauty of God's creation, there is a comforting awareness of the fact that as Creator of the heavens and earth, He is still in control and sits on the throne. It also causes me to realize that He has a purpose in the things He allows. I trust Him with the outcome of my life as I walk with Him each day, confident that all of my tomorrows are planned by His love. I'm more aware of the truth that as *my* Creator He fashioned me for His glory, uniquely designed to become a reflection of His light and life on this earth. With that realization has come grace to trust His love for me and rest in His sovereign plan, knowing He will fulfill His wonderful purpose for my life.

Chapter 4

His Strength in our Weakness

As far as human weaknesses are concerned, mine are many, but God tells us in His Word that His grace is sufficient for us because in those very weaknesses His strength is perfected and the fruit of His nature developed within us. His love and grace come shining through. The wonderful thing is, His strength is grown in the soil of our weaknesses. As we submit them and our fears to Him in prayer, asking Him to bring the transforming power of His Spirit to live in that area, we will receive greater grace to gain victory over ourselves. We will begin to experience the reality and power of Christ living within us and the joy of being led by His Spirit. We will experientially realize that our only source of strength is in Him alone, that without Him we can do nothing.

I love what the apostle Paul revealed about his own weaknesses as he penned the words that when he was weak, then he was strong because the power of Christ rested upon him (was demonstrated in him). Of all the apostles, Paul is my favorite because he was so humble and transparent about his weaknesses.

This is of great encouragement to me. It lets me know we should remember to thank God for them, because it is through our struggles we are brought to our knees in the realization that we have nothing to bring Him but empty hands and a humbled heart. Sometimes it is through our failures that we are brought to an acute awareness of our need for complete dependency upon His grace and the transforming power of His Spirit to change us.

In Psalm 51:17 (NIV), we see a picture of the only kind of sacrifice we can offer God that moves His heart and gets His attention: *"The sacrifices of God are a broken spirit, a broken and a contrite heart, O God, you will not despise."* Nothing less than honesty and humility before the throne of grace is acceptable to God. Where there is no change of heart or attitude, there is no true repentance, regardless of outward conformity to religious standards or acts of service performed in the name of Christ.

If service is not rendered from a sincere heart of love for Him and the ones we are serving, it is nothing less than "performance." God wants the real you, all of you, not just an external façade without the inward substance of a true heart relationship with God through Jesus Christ. In II Timothy 3:5 (NIV), this counterfeit Christianity is described as *"having a form of godliness but denying its power."*

There was no middle ground or fence walking for Paul. From the moment Saul, the persecutor of the church, encountered Christ and the sudden realization of Who He is, his heart was broken, his direction changed abruptly, and his heart was fully surrendered to the One he had persecuted. From that moment on his life was forever changed from Saul (his Jewish name) to become Paul, the apostle of the Lord Jesus Christ to the Gentiles. Because of his persecution of the church, he considered himself the least of all the apostles. He had many struggles with his weaknesses in the process of becoming like his Lord and the man God saw and created him to be. Researching Paul's background left me amazed at how one encounter with the Lord Jesus Christ left his physical eyes blinded in order to open his spiritual eyes to see the real purpose for which he was born.

He was a Jew, whose father was of the strictest sect of the Jews, a Pharisee of the tribe of Benjamin, and also a Roman citizen. He grew up in the city of Tarsus, the capital of Cilicia, a Roman province in Asia Minor. Because of its location, the city became the center of extensive commercial traffic and distinguished for the wealth of its inhabitants. It was also the seat of a famous university, higher in reputation even than the universities of Athens and Alexandria. Here he spent his youth, enjoying the best education the city could provide. He was later educated in Jerusalem where he studied law under the highly respected rabbi, Gamaliel, and spent years in an elaborate study of the Scriptures. He became a zealous nationalist and a Pharisee.

Coming from this background of legal and religious superiority, Saul in his blindness thought he was doing God a favor by persecuting Christians, until the life-altering encounter with the living Christ which opened his eyes to see the truth about himself and the persecution he was bringing against the Lord.

In much of what I've read about him, Paul is often depicted as a powerful and eloquent orator—and indeed he was, in the matters of legal and scriptural debates from his years of training and education. However, after his encounter with the Lord, Paul paints a different picture of himself because he "saw" that none of his education, background, or position made him acceptable to God and there was nothing he could do to earn God's grace or favor or merit eternal life. The foundation of wealth, education, and religious status on which he had built his life crumbled into nothing and He was thrust into complete dependency upon the Lord to empower him to preach the gospel to the Gentiles, the message of God's saving grace through Jesus Christ. He writes in Ephesians 2:8,9 (NIV): *"For it is by grace you have been saved, through faith, and this not from yourselves, it is the gift of God, not by works, so that no one can boast."* In his own words as I read the verses from Romans 7:15, 24, 25 (NIV), and in I Corinthians chapters 1 and 2 (NIV), my understanding has been opened to see a different picture of this man whom God used so mightily to spread the gospel and change lives—in the midst of his struggles with human weakness. Perhaps it speaks to me because I relate more to weakness than to strength. I hope the following verses will help paint a different picture of his humanity and the reality of his struggles in the process of becoming the man God called him to be, to fulfill all of his calling and destiny in Christ Jesus:

"...for what I want to do I do not do, but what I hate I do. What a wretched man I am! Who will rescue me from this body of death? Thanks be to God, through Jesus Christ our Lord!" (Romans 7:15, 24, 25 (NIV)

"When I came to you, brothers, I did not come with eloquence or superior wisdom as I proclaimed to you the testimony about God. For I resolved to know nothing while I was with you except Jesus Christ and him crucified. I came to you in weakness and fear, and with much trembling. My message and my preaching were not with wise and persuasive words, but with a demonstration of the Spirit's power, so that your faith might not rest on men's wisdom, but on God's power." I Corinthians 2:1-5 (NIV)

"Brothers, think of what you were when you were called. Not many of you were wise by human standards; not many were influential; not many were of noble birth. But God chose the foolish things of the world to shame the wise; God chose the weak things of the world to shame the strong. He chose the lowly things of this world and the despised things—and the things that are not—to nullify the things that are, so that no one may boast before him. It is because of him that you are in Christ Jesus, who has become for us wisdom from God—that is, our

righteousness, holiness and redemption. Therefore, as it is written: 'Let him who boasts boast in the Lord.'" I Corinthians 1:26-31 (NIV)

When I first received the Lord as my Savior, my favorite Scripture verses were Proverbs 3:5,6, which basically instruct us to trust in the Lord with all our hearts, not to lean on our own understanding, and as we follow Him in all our ways He will direct our steps. Those are still among my favorite verses. However, as I experienced life's trials in which God began to expose and deal with my self-will and fears, I discovered how much I needed Him, how weak I was and am without Him. The truth of the above-quoted Scriptures from I Corinthians have become my verses to live by.

We never know until we are put under pressure what our hidden flaws and weaknesses are. God uses pressure to reveal to us what is in us, what is not in us, and how much more of Him we need. He uses these times to show us that sometimes we are not really where we think we are in our walk with Him. With certainty, what is in us will come out of us. When we find ourselves in situations that are beyond our ability or strength to handle, as we turn to Him in confession of our need, He will supply the grace and strength to help us through. He is always there for us.

He uses such situations to bring us to the end of our self-sufficiency and to our knees. Now, each day, I am acutely aware that without Him I can do nothing, and my only strength is in Him and through Him. Truly, the only boast any of us can make is about Him, the wonder of His unconditional love, grace, and the price He paid to redeem us.

When you are young, you live and operate in your natural strength because God gave you the energy of youth and it is lived each day without a thought for there is nothing from which to draw a comparison. For those of you who are still in your youth, you will not be able to relate to what has taken me a lifetime to learn. I remember well those days of my youth. However, as we grow older and our youthful strength and energy fade, we slow to a lesser pace, and begin to realize how necessary it is for us to daily draw our strength and life from the power of Christ's life within us. When Jesus died on the cross, He gave His life *for* us, but when He resurrected from the dead, He gave His life *to* us. When Jesus rose from the dead and ascended into heaven, He sent the Holy Spirit to live *within* us. It is through His Spirit living within that we can ask for and appropriate each day a fresh supply of His life and power for our spirit, soul and body. This is a truth that *so* needs to be understood, believed and appropriated by believers everywhere, a truth which only His Spirit can reveal to individual hearts.

Now that I am older, as I begin each day with God spending time in His presence, not only do I ask for, but literally depend upon, a fresh filling with His Spirit and a deposit of His resurrection life and power for the day. Not only do I desire His life and power within this mortal body, but I *require* it in order to live the life He gave me. There is nothing left for me apart from His life within.

In Romans 8:11 (NIV) it says: *"And if the Spirit of him who raised Jesus from the dead is living in you, he who raised Christ from the dead will also give life to your mortal bodies through his Spirit, who lives in you."*

He truly is my resurrection and my life. I'm so thankful that He fills me with fresh life, strength, and purpose for each day!

If you can relate to what has been shared here and consider yourself among the weak, I encourage you to read the Scripture again, I Corinthians 1:26-31, and take heart from its message. Not many mighty ones has God chosen, not many wise or of noble birth, but He has chosen the weak, the lowly, and the willing through whom He accomplishes great things for His glory.

Chapter 5

Seasons

As this chapter is being written, it is winter here in Idaho, a chilly thirty-six degrees with a forecast of rain and snow for tomorrow. Even though winter is not my favorite time of year because of the cold and gray stormy skies, I do love it here where we enjoy the four seasons. Fortunately, our winters in the Treasure Valley are pretty mild compared to other areas up north.

As one looks at the trees with their branches stripped bare, they appear to be dead with no life in them. However, quite the opposite is true, for this is the time a tree's roots draw deeply from the life-giving nutrients in the soil, carrying them up into every branch and fiber of the tree in preparation for new growth in the spring. Though outwardly dormant and in a season of rest, it is still full of life.

When I think of the natural seasons of earth, it reminds me of the truth that just as there are seasons of nature, so there are seasons of change in our lives. Just as in nature, so in our lives one season follows another, each bringing its own purpose. There are seasons of rest, pruning, growth, and fruitfulness.

I love using the analogy of trees and their growth. If one were to study the history of a huge tree and its environment, it would have a story to tell. From the time trees are planted as a tiny seed, sprouting up as a seedling, surviving the elements of weather conditions, disease and fire, some grow into strong and majestic monarchs. You can see how it carries lessons for our lives.

When I see a beautiful old tree that has survived storms and lashing winds, whose roots have gone down deep into the soil and rocks beneath, it speaks so loudly to me of life itself and how many times it takes the hardships we experience to produce strength and proven character in us. If we look to God and put our roots down deep in Him, drawing nutrients from His Word will cause us to grow strong in the adversities of life.

In Psalm 62:2 (NKJV) the psalmist declares: *"He only is my rock and my salvation; He is my defense; I shall not be greatly moved."* In the winter of our soul, the deep places in God's heart call to the deep places in ours. It is the perfect time to seek Him for a deeper relationship.

Sometimes adversity brings us to a sudden stop where we are forced to evaluate our life purpose and what is really important.

Winter Rest

If things you were once engaged in are no longer productive or bring joy, if certain activities have come to an end and doors close in places of service or in friendships you value, if you're suffering from broken relationships, exhaustion or "burn out", what you're experiencing is a season of winter in which the only way of recouping is rest.

If you have a relationship with God, He will use everything in your life to teach and strengthen you. His aim is to build in you a place of deeper dependency upon Him where you will draw from the strength of His life. From there He will be able to bring you to a place of rest and trust in Him. Each season is preparation for the next. If you don't have a relationship with Him, you can be sure He wants to reveal Himself and His love for you where you are.

We live in a culture that is always geared around constant activity where we are doing and going, and, unfortunately, we don't know what it is to rest. Even in the church, if we're not engaged in projects and on the go, we feel guilty because we're not *doing*. We were created to be human *beings*, not human *doings*. Even God rested on the seventh day after He created the world.

So, if you find yourself experiencing the exhaustion of too much busyness in your life, be aware of the fact that even as God is in control of the seasons of nature, so He is in control of the seasons of your life. He desires to bring you to a new place of rest and renewal. It would be wise to ask Him to help you recognize what season He is bringing you into, and His *purpose* in it, then *yield* to His will, and *cooperate* with Him in it. Remember, rest is the preparation for new growth in the spring. He wants to give you wisdom and understanding so you may grow and flourish in every season of life—and *that includes rest*.

Spring Pruning

Following every winter, anyone who has trees to care for knows its pruning time—a very necessary part of preparing the trees for the new and healthy growth for greater fruitfulness in the spring. The old growth hinders the new life and needs to be cut away. What once contained life is now dead. Where our lives are concerned, Jesus compares us to branches of a vine. He says in John 15:1,2 (NIV):

"I am the true vine, and my Father is the gardner. He cuts off every branch in me that bears no fruit, while every branch that does bear fruit he prunes so that it will be even more fruitful."

It is as true in the spiritual realm as it is in the natural. When God prunes us, He cuts off the old things that once had life in them, but no longer do. The activities or even service in the church or other places where we have given of ourselves for the benefit of others no longer bring us joy or have the sense of "life" and productiveness in them. It is a time when we need to lay those activities aside and let God take away the things He no longer wants in our lives. He sometimes removes good things in order to bring something better.

When the old is removed, it means He is preparing to do a new and greater work in us, and it is essential to recognize this, cooperating with Him in it. If we still cling to the old things and places of involvement when He is desiring to give us new direction, it will keep us focused on the old so we're not ready to receive or even look for the new thing He is wanting to bring forth. The good can sometimes be the enemy of His best. He wants us to be in tune with Him, and learn to come into alignment with His plan and purposes. Again, I emphasize the need to ask God to reveal to you what He is doing and help you understand what He wants.

In Psalm 119:73 (NIV) the psalmist prays: *"Your hands made me and formed me; give me understanding to learn your commands."* There are no shortcuts in the pruning process. When God prunes us, it hurts. The ending of things, loss of a relationship through conflict, death, or divorce, or other disappointment is not without pain. However, the thing that hurts most is when we stubbornly cling to that which is dead and fruitless. Letting go will bring us a sense of relief and eventually will lead to new life. This is what spring does. It brings forth new life. It always speaks of new beginnings and fresh hope.

Summer Fruit

Summer brings a profusion of life and fruitfulness. The buds of new life which appeared in the spring have now blossomed to produce an abundance of fruit. So, in our lives, there is greater productivity as we share with others the life of joyful service from His love which He produced in us from the preceding season of being pruned. We find ourselves changed, freed from some old mindsets and things or relationships we used to cling to. Now we are able to enjoy the new life of service with fresh joy and renewed enthusiasm. This is also a new season—a busy but wonderful season. Summer is alive with activity and fruitfulness as we enjoy being in community with others. I relish the warmer and longer days, the sunshine and early morning walks along the greenbelt near my home. Each day's walk is a time of thanksgiving and praise to my Creator for the gift of the day and His presence with me. It is exhilarating to see and hear the sounds of nature, the birds and their various songs, the sound of the water as it flows over the rocks in the brook. My heart is filled with joy as I reminisce and reflect on the goodness of God!

Autumn Color

Autumn—my favorite time of the year because of its breathtaking beauty, the trees and shrubs in their full dress of brilliant colors. When the leaves turn, my favorite thing to do is take a drive to McCall and tour around the lake, or visit Garden Valley and drink in the view. The crisp autumn air is invigorating to walk in and gives me fresh perspective and quietness in which to reflect upon God's handiwork and the beauty of the colors all around me.

One year when my husband's job required him to deliver a load of wood to a small town in Montana, I accompanied him on the trip in October. I can only try to describe the brilliant colors of the trees we encountered as we drove through the valley. I've never witnessed anything so beautiful and breathtaking. The mountains on all sides were clothed in their full dress of gold, brilliant red, and orange, the yellow of the tamarack trees among the green of the pines. The entire scene was a tapestry of color as far as the eye could see on both sides of the highway.

We were privileged to make another delivery in the same area two weeks later, and the colors were even more brilliant than they were earlier. During that trip God was teaching me about seasons in relation to my life with Him. He was showing me from His beautiful creation that He saves His best for last; though it is late in my life, it is not too late for Him to fulfill His purpose and plan for me. It was a trip full of promise which renewed my hope that the best was yet to be.

It's All Good

Wherever you are in life, whatever season, there is hope for your future, and God does have a plan for you and desires to fulfill His dream and purpose for your life. Though it may be late in time, and you may feel like you've missed His will, yet He is faithful to take your life as you place it in His hands and say, "Here I am Lord, use me." Even though you may think you have nothing to offer God, or think your life is so small He can't use you, He will take your "little" and multiply it into "much" when you give Him all you are and all you have. God can and will do miracles through one small life placed in His hands.

Every life is made up of seasons from which we can grow and learn to know the One Who created us for His pleasure. In every life there is pain and pleasure, sorrow and joy, loss and gain. I have learned that every season is an opportunity to learn to know and love the One Who knows and loves us best.

In every season He is always present with us with a desire to reveal Himself and more of His love to us. Your life is a story being written with a purpose to fulfill and each day is a fresh, blank page on which your story will continue. Your choices will determine what is written there. His hand of love is always reaching. His purpose is in every season. It is so true that *"to everything there is a season, a time for every purpose under heaven."* Ecclesiastes 3:1 (NKJV)

Chapter 6

Bouquet from Heaven

It was a gray and dreary day, December 28, 2002. I remember the date so well because I was experiencing depression. The only word to describe my feelings that day is "insignificant." It was a day I'll never forget, because it was a defining moment in my life in which God forever changed my perspective of myself and of Him as my Creator. It was an encounter in which my Creator revealed Himself to me in a new, personal, and miraculous way as my Father.

As I was walking from our house to the garage where my husband was working in his shop, little pieces of snow began to fall on the walk in front of me for about eight or ten feet in diameter around me. At first I thought they were just pieces of sleet, but in my curiosity I bent down and scooped a few into my hand. To my surprise, upon closer examination, I saw each one was a miniature cone-shaped chunk with the perfect design of a daisy embossed on the top! Having difficulty believing what I was seeing, I gathered some more from several feet away, and every one was exactly the same! They were no bigger around than a pencil eraser and perfectly cone shaped, each one with the same daisy imprint on top.

I gathered a few in my hand and opened the door to the garage, showed them to my husband, and he just shook his head in amazement. The ground all around the area where the snow "flowers" fell was entirely dry, our front and back yard, and the neighbors; every other place was completely dry. In those moments as I held some more of the quickly melting flowers in my hand, the Lord spoke to my heart a very strong and clear message of truth that I so desperately needed to hear. In a moment of time, He interrupted the natural process of falling snow and created a bouquet which spoke directly to my heart. It was as if He stooped down and handed it to me with these words: "You think you're insignificant? Here, Ruthie, this is from My heart to yours. No child of Mine ever goes unnoticed, is ever insignificant, unloved or uncared for by their Heavenly Father."

At the impact of those words, I had to find a place to sit in quiet amazement and wonder at the miracle I had just experienced! I was speechless for some time as my thoughts were so filled with a keen awareness of His presence and love. It left an indelible imprint on my heart to think that our God and Creator would intervene in the order of nature to create a bouquet of ice flowers for me, His child, to express His love for me. They let me know I am of great significance and value to Him. It was a miraculous reminder sent by His hand at a time when my heart was in desperate need of His touch.

Though this miracle was sent to me, it contains a message for every person. The truth is, God created each of us with great significance and value. The value He has placed on us was expressed in the giving of His all for us, the cost of His Son's life on the cross. We are the most valued and cherished of all His creation. God still does miraculous things today, and if we are not too busy with the fast pace of living, if we slow down, we may be fortunate enough to witness and experience them when we least expect it, and in ways we would never dream of. God is a lover of simplicity and beauty and longs to communicate His love to us through the simple beauties of His created world if we will purposely take notice and be aware of it. There is not a child of His that goes unnoticed by Him. He knows the individual needs of each of us and longs to communicate His love in ways that are unique to each person.

I've thought about that experience many times and it warms my heart to recall the way in which God in a moment of time took notice of my need and expressed His love to me with that "bouquet" of His creation. It still leaves me in awe and causes me to say, "Wow!" I've also thought how easy it would have been to miss that miracle. If I had been busy with other things or people and not been there in the place where God wanted to meet me, I would have missed a miracle. It causes me to wonder if there have been times I've been too busy and so unaware of God's presence that I've missed Him and the blessing He wanted to give me. When we're in a hurry, we miss much of what is important in life. It's easy to attend to the urgent things but let the important things go, such as our relationships with our Creator and those He has placed in our lives to love.

Throughout our lives there will be events and things that will bring defining moments to us, moments in which our hearts are touched and changed. I don't want to miss any of those moments that God has for me in which to experience His love for me and to love Him more deeply, to know Him more intimately. He is always longing to meet with us, to reveal more of Himself and Who He is to us. His majesty, glory, and wonder of His creation are all around us if our eyes could only be opened to see! My prayer is often, "Lord, open my eyes to see You more clearly, and the expressions of Yourself in the beauty of creation. Please don't let me miss You and what You want me to see. Please show me Your glory!"

****

My prayer for anyone reading this is that your spirit would be stirred and awakened to desire God Himself above and beyond any other goal in life, that you will seek Him with all your heart. If you will seek Him, you will find Him when you search for Him with all your heart. And He will be found by you because His heart longs to make Himself known to you. He loves you so! May He make this truth a reality in your heart.

Chapter 7

Storms

As I sit here looking through the window at the gray storm clouds and watching the branches of the pine tree sway in the wind, I notice the mourning dove who built her nest there sitting securely and calmly through it all. The wind and rain outside remind me of God's faithfulness to protect His children in the midst of any storm and I am embraced by His presence, at rest in the realization of His hand of protection. Just as surely as He has power and authority over the forces of nature and all of His creation, yet cares for and provides for the birds, so, too, is He in control of my life and watches over me. As His child I am of more value to Him than the birds. This is the place of rest into which He has brought me, and I am at peace in the assurance of His love and care, trusting that underneath me are His everlasting arms. I rest in His faithfulness.

I am in process, as is everyone reading this book. This place of trust and rest is the work He has accomplished in my heart, which, sad to say, has been produced only through times of crises, the storms in life which forced me to a place of complete dependency upon Him. It has taken brokenness of heart and will, broken dreams and loss which put me on my face before His cross—prostrate, depleted, helpless, yielded, waiting for the merciful touch of His Spirit to breathe new life into my being and lift me to my feet once again. There have been many such times in my life, much breaking and loss, and by His grace a resurrection to new life again with a deeper trust in Him. Because He has shown Himself to be my place of refuge and strength as a very present help in time of trouble, I have learned to rest and trust in Him. In every situation God has revealed to me His love, tenderness, mercy, and grace to heal and restore.

Oh, our soul power dies hard! By that I mean *our* will, *our* emotions, *our* thoughts that always want to be in control—but die we must to these things if we are ever to be transformed into the person God designed and created us to be. That can only happen if we make Jesus the Lord of our lives. If He is ever to be glorified in us and His love flow through us, we must be willing to die to our own ways and desires.

Again, I am reminded of the Apostle Paul and his words to the Galatian believers: *"I have been crucified with Christ; it is no longer I who live, but Christ lives in me; and the life which I now live in the flesh I live by faith in the Son of God, who loved me and gave Himself for me."* Gal. 2:20 (NKJV). How did he come to this place of wholehearted surrender and abandonment to Christ? Through the opposition and trials he experienced, which I like to refer to as storms. The turbulent times and dangerous situations he encountered forced him to rely on and trust his life completely to his Lord. I'm confident that during these times of struggle in his life, his weaknesses all too often surfaced to cause him grief. But they also drove him to a deeper dependency upon Christ's strength and transforming grace to change him.

Have you ever asked God the question, "Why?" Why does God allow things to come into our lives that rip our hearts apart and turn our world upside down? I don't know of a person who hasn't at some point asked Him that question.

I have.

Sometimes He has given me insight into His purpose, but a lot of the time He has left me to depend on and learn to trust Him in the situation, realizing His greatest aim is to develop Christ's character in me. He allows a storm or trial in my life to bring me into a deeper relationship with Himself and to demonstrate His faithfulness, which brings honor to His name.

Now my prayer is, "Lord, change ME, create in me a heart like Yours and help me be faithful to You." I'm learning to trust in the knowledge of His love for me as His child, remembering that my life belongs to Him. He has promised to work things out for my good and His purpose. His Word has been and is my compass in life on which I rely daily for guidance. Psalm 119:105 (NKJV) is one of my favorites: *"Your word is a lamp to my feet and a light to my path."*

God doesn't always let us know why we go through the experiences which come to us, at least not at the time, and usually not until much later, sometimes never. There will always be some things left unanswered, known only to Him. We live in a fallen, sin-sick world in which the choices of others affect us and also those around us. In everything that happens to us, we have a choice as to what will happen in us. The troubles we experience will either make us better or bitter. God cares about what happens to us, but is more concerned about what happens within us, more concerned about our transformation than our comfort and ease. Transformation requires our willingness to change, and change is hard. It will require courage and the renewal of our mind. Romans 12:2 (NKJV)

There is insight and wisdom for living contained in the Word of God which applies to our daily life experiences if we will seek the help it affords. Without knowledge of His Word we cannot learn or know His ways. In study and experience I find there is much God wants to teach us. There is so much more He wants to give us of Himself, His love and presence, and the riches of His grace. These are conditional upon our willingness and desire to seek Him as our first priority in life. He will not waste anything we go through if we turn our life and circumstances over to Him, letting Him have His way, working things out His way, one day at a time. The big question is, *do we love Him enough to let Him have our hearts and lives, and will we trust Him enough to follow Him?*

Years ago, when we lived in New Mexico and our children were still at home, we wanted to spend the day with the kids. So we took a drive to Albuquerque on a Saturday to do some Christmas shopping. I was resting on the couch in the van with my Bible, reading about Paul's shipwreck. In my mind I was picturing the painting of a ship in a storm which we had hanging in our living room. As I read through the chapter, the Lord spoke to my heart about our family, that our family unit would suffer shipwreck but all the souls on board would be saved. I realized that God was giving me that understanding to prepare me for the future. I held those thoughts in my heart because I didn't want to believe it, and certainly didn't speak of it.

However, in time it proved to be true as I watched our family fracture and pull apart, despite my efforts to hold us all together. I had to release all of us to God, trusting Him to finish the work He had begun in each of our lives. I had to come to the place of absolute trust in God's faithfulness to fulfill what He had promised—to save every member of my family.

For a better picture of Paul's shipwreck and God's rescue of all souls on board, I encourage you to read about this exciting account in Acts 27. From that event in Paul's life, I Peter 1:3-9, and in Romans 12:2, and what I've learned through personal experience in life and loss, God not only desires to save us, but desires to achieve several objectives within us. These valuable principles can help serve as an anchor to hold you steady during a time of crisis.

STORMS - THEIR PURPOSES

I find three basic reasons for the storms in our lives:

Opposition

First is opposition. When we are serving the Lord and are in the center of His will, we will sometimes encounter human opposition and also at times opposition from the destructive forces of satan and the kingdom of darkness. An important factor is to realize that we have an enemy because we live in a fallen, sin-infested world, and as Jesus' words in John 10:10 (NKJV) tell us: *"The thief does not come except to steal, and to kill, and to destroy."* There is no avoiding it. It is part of the cost of being a true disciple of Christ and sharing in the fellowship of His sufferings. And Jesus went on to say, *"I have come that they may have life, and that they may have it more abundantly."* Other Scripture tells us: *"Dear friends, do not be surprised at the painful trial you are suffering, as though something strange were happening to you, but rejoice that you participate in the sufferings of Christ, so that you may be overjoyed when His glory is revealed."* I Peter 4:12,13

Purification

Second, storms are allowed to purify us. I Peter 1:7 (NKJV) tells us: *"These have come so that your faith—of greater worth than gold, which perishes even though refined by fire—may be proved genuine and may result in praise, glory and honor when Jesus Christ is revealed."*

Please read 1 Peter 1:3-9. As gold is heated and melted in the fire, so the impurities within us come to the surface and become visible. We can only deal with what we are able to see. Job 23:10 (NKJV) says:

"But He knows the way that I take; when he has tested me, I will come forth as gold."

Transformation

Third, to transform us. God is more interested in transforming us than in our comfort. You may have heard the saying that God loves us just the way we are but loves us too much to leave us that way. So true. Romans 12:2 (NIV) instructs us: *"Do not conform any longer to the pattern of this world, but be transformed by the renewing of your mind. Then you will be able to test and approve what God's will is—his good, pleasing and perfect will."* Ephesians 4:23,24 (NIV) states: *"to be made new in the attitude of your minds; and to put on the new self, created to be like God in true righteousness and holiness."* The only way we can be transformed is by having our minds changed to think differently, and that can only happen through reading the Word of God coupled with our prayer asking Him to change us. He will faithfully meet us when we desire and are willing to be changed. God uses the heat of trials to purify us, and our struggles to transform us.

ANCHORS IN THE STORMS - HIS PROVISIONS

His Presence

The first anchor for survival is *being aware of His presence and then turning to Him* Who is our hope. The Lord's presence is always here with us in the midst of the storm. In the situation described in Matthew 14:22-31, Jesus came walking on the water to the disciples as they were in the boat on a storm-tossed sea. They thought He was a ghost and were terrified. His presence and power were there to strengthen, protect and help them, but they were terrified for two reasons, the first being that they were overwhelmed by the storm's intensity and their own helplessness to survive it. The second was that they were not expecting to see Jesus, and didn't recognize Him when they did.

We are no different than they were, so given to fear in overwhelming circumstances, so prone to forget that He is always here with us in every situation desiring to help if we will remember to look to Him. His words to them in their storm are still His words for us today in ours. The moment they cried out to Him, He spoke: *"Be of good cheer! It is I, do not be afraid."* Matthew 14:27 (NKJV) Our peace is not in the storm, but in Jesus Himself. Looking to Him in the midst of it will help bring calm out of chaos and the comfort of His presence. He has promised never to leave or forsake us. Hebrews 13:5 (NKJV) When you realize His presence in the storm, it can lead you to a deeper level of trust where you will experience His peace.

Our Prayers

Acts 27 describes the desperate situation in which Paul and those traveling with him found themselves. In verses 20-29, it is clear that Paul prayed and God spared all those who sailed with him; also in their fear they prayed. Luke 18:1-8 describes the importance of specific and persistent prayers and how God honors them when they are from honest and desperate hearts. I Thessalonians 5:17,18 and Philippians 4:6,7 tell us to pray continually, bringing every fear and concern to Him with thanksgiving. In James 5:16 we are promised that if we confess our sins to one another and pray for each other, we will be healed; also that the prayer of a righteous person is powerful and effective. There are many verses that urge us to pray continually. In Acts 12 Peter is in prison, the entire church prayed for him, and God intervened by sending an angel to release him from prison.

Prayer is simply honest, and sometimes desperate, dialogue with God, not a form of words learned from others, but voicing *your* thoughts and needs to Him in *your own words* as a child would come to a parent, but with a thankful heart. He honors simple and sincere prayers and it is His desire that we come to Him with every need. That is the first step in entering into a relationship with Him, turning to and talking with Him, confessing our need for Him, asking Jesus to forgive our sins and be the Savior and Lord of our lives. I've heard people say that God doesn't talk to them. The key to hearing from Him is first talking to Him, then *listening*.

When we seek Him and are quiet and still, He will sometimes drop a thought quietly into our spirit, giving us direction. Or sometimes He speaks directly to us words of hope or instruction from the Scriptures. Also, He sometimes speaks to us by allowing us to see His active intervention in our circumstances. We will know His voice by His peace. Many times when I hear someone say they don't hear from God, its possible they are not listening, their minds being filled with life's busyness and many distractions. The only other reason for not hearing from Him is if we love and hold on to sin in our hearts. Psalm 66:18-20 (NIV) says:

"If I had cherished sin in my heart, the Lord would not have listened; but God has surely listened and heard my voice in prayer. Praise be to God, who has not rejected my prayer or withheld his love from me!"

I believe one of the greatest hindrances to prayer is busyness and the neglect of purposely seeking God, by setting aside time to be with Him in prayer and reading His Word. Jesus' life was constantly filled with people who had needs and He would get up before daylight to go away to spend time with His Father. He knew He needed that time alone with His Father to pray, to hear what He was saying, and what the desires of His heart were toward the people; also, he needed physical and spiritual strengthening for each new day.

If Jesus, who is God's Son and Savior of the world, needed time alone with His Father to be strengthened, renewed, and to gain direction for each day, then how much more do we! No greater gift could you give to Him than to desire and make time to spend with Him, as you would for a best friend.

It's an awesome reality that our Creator and Holy God invites and desires your presence. But He does! He invites you to come to the throne of grace. We can approach Him with confidence because of the shed blood of His Son, our Savior Jesus Christ, whose sacrifice paid for and forgave all our sins. His heart longs to meet with you. He loves you so! Won't you come? *"Let us therefore come boldly to the throne of grace, that we may obtain mercy and find grace to help in time of need."* Hebrews 4:18 (NKJV)

STORMS – HIS PROMISES

The Bible is true, and its promises are many, but most are conditional upon our faith. I could relate many of them here, but will only list a few that are some of my favorites. These are engraved in my memory and are a constant source of encouragement and strength to my faith.

Jeremiah 29:11-13 (NKJV) states:

"For I know the thoughts that I think toward you, says the Lord, thoughts of peace and not of evil, to give you a future and a hope. Then you will call upon Me and go and pray to Me and I will listen to you. And you will seek Me and find Me, when you search for Me with all your heart."

Other favorites which emphasize the absolute necessity of faith are:

John 3:16,17 (NKJV): *"For God so loved the world that He gave His only begotten Son, that whoever believes in Him should not perish but have everlasting life. For God did not send His Son into the world to condemn the world, but that the world through Him might be saved."*

Hebrews 11:6 (NKJV) says: *"But without faith it is impossible to please Him, for he who comes to God must believe that He is, and that He is a rewarder of those who diligently seek Him."*

Hebrews 6:11,12 (NKJV: *"And we desire that each one of you show the same diligence to the full assurance of hope until the end, that you do not become sluggish, but imitate those who through faith and patience inherit the promises."*

And one in which I find great comfort and encouragement is I John 1:9 (NKJV): *"If we confess our sins, He is faithful and just to forgive us our sins and to cleanse us from all unrighteousness."*

These are but a few that have transformed my life as I have meditated upon and memorized them. God's Word is life and cleansing for our minds and hearts.

Jesus said of His words: *"My words are Spirit and they are life."* His promises are a weapon against the enemy of our souls, satan and his lies, because God's Word is true.

Jesus is the living Word, He is the truth, and His words stand forever. In Mark 13:31 (NKJV) He states: *"Heaven and earth will pass away, but My words will by no means pass away."* Believing and trusting His Word in times of crisis is so vital to maintaining stability and spiritual equilibrium to see you through the worst of times so your faith will not be shipwrecked.

We must learn to walk by faith, not by sight, because the externals of what we see in our circumstances are temporary. What is not seen is eternal. II Corinthians 4:17,18 (NKJV) tells us:

"For our light affliction which is but for a moment, is working for us a far more exceeding and eternal weight of glory, while we do not look at the things which are seen, but at the things which are not seen. For the things which are seen are temporary, but the things which are not seen are eternal."

May your faith be encouraged by these words of truth.

Chapter 8

Legacy

On July 18, 1954, David Martin Knoblock entered this world in Prescott, Arizona, weighing in at seven pounds, eleven ounces, nineteen and a half inches long. He was strong, a beautiful boy with auburn brown hair and brown eyes. It seems in my memories it was a short time ago, yet it's been a lifetime.

Today is January 15, 2010, and the date reminds me of my oldest son, David, and his death on April 15, 2008, passing from this life to the ultimate life in heaven, to dwell in the very presence of his Heavenly Father forever. He was 53 years old. As I wrote today's date in my journal and thought about David's death, which I refer to as his graduation to glory, my eyes fell on the quote at the bottom of the page. It reminded me of the truth that the most holy and glorious promises of God are sometimes fulfilled in a manner we would never choose. In seeing His child's deepest need, He reaches down to save him at a time when circumstances look just the opposite, when feelings defy that possibility because our hearts are torn with loss.

As I replayed his life and death in my memories, it was a mixture of sadness and joy as my heart was filled with a prayer of thanksgiving to God which I wrote as my offering of praise. This is my prayer: "The quote on this page for today reminds me of how wise You are in the way You sometimes choose to rescue Your children from circumstances beyond their ability to endure and continue in. I think of David and how tired and weary he had become, spiritually and physically—his love for You and his family, the people he knew and worked with, the life and legacy of love he left all over this valley. Thank You for the man You helped him become—a journey through much darkness, personal pain and struggle, to a victorious life which honored You and which honored me. Thank You for such a gift! He honored You in life and in death he graduated to glory with honors. I honor his memory. Thank You for Your goodness and mercy in taking him home to be in Your presence forever."

A few days after his death, my heart was asking God to give me something that would comfort me. I wasn't angry because I knew with assurance that God never makes a mistake, but I needed a word from Him that would give me some under-standing. A card came in the mail from a friend in which were two verses of Scripture giving me a picture of God's heart for my son as to why he had to go. It was a huge comfort. The verses were Isaiah 57:1,2 (NIV):

"The righteous perish, and no one ponders it in his heart; devout men are taken away, and no one understands that the righteous are taken away to be spared from evil. Those who walk uprightly enter into peace; they find rest as they lie in death."

These words still give me much comfort and fill my heart with thankfulness. I imagine God in His great love for David must have reached down and taken him by the hand and said something like "It's enough, you've done well, son, it's time to come home."

On April 11, 2008, David collapsed at work as he was unloading some heavy wood from his truck. He had just finished nailing the last board on a remodel he was doing. He always insisted that no job should ever be left unfinished. He was rushed to the hospital; he had suffered a stroke which paralyzed the left side of his body. That very morning he had called me to say he loved and appreciated me, and ended with his usual cheerful blessing, "God bless your day, Mom."

On the third day, he rallied and began moving his left leg, arm, and fingers. When the nurse came in to check him that Sunday morning, David greeted him and told the nurse he was better. All that day, little miracles took place. He was able to tell each of us he loved us, and visit a little. He managed to walk himself on a walker to the chair beside a nearby window, enjoying the sun shining through. Everyone we knew was joining us in prayer for his recovery. Even the doctor who was a skeptic said she thought we had our miracle, that he was going to pull through.

The progress was short-lived because Monday he was not responding to any of us or attempts by the nurse to make him move his toes. We had just arrived home on Monday evening when the hospital called and told us to come back because his brain was bleeding and he was dying. We each were able to tell him we loved him and say the things that were on our hearts. At 1:55 a.m. on April 15th, his great heart stopped.

There are a lot of wonderful memories of David. He was so full of life and had such a great sense of humor! From the time he was little, he loved to make people laugh, tell jokes and funny stories. We often told him he should have been a clown, and he was truly funny. The sound effects he used to make of screeching brakes and crashes would always bring us to attention and his voice impressions of Disney characters were hilarious. He kept us laughing. He never knew a stranger.

The story he fabricated about me years ago still lives today and seems to be one of those family legends that never die. When he was a teenager, our church had invited a preacher from out of town to conduct a week of meetings, so families in the church opened our homes to share meals with him. As we were enjoying dinner together, David posed the question to him, "Did you know my mom used to skate in the roller derby?" And the story went from there, growing bigger with each statement. My husband went right along with David's wild story, both of them very serious in their expressions and very convincing—and all the while I'm vehemently protesting, "Not true! Not true!" We all had laughs over it and it was an enjoyable evening.

I thought no more about it and assumed that was the end of it. However, a couple of nights later at the meeting, after the singing was finished and before the preacher gave his message, he made an announcement to the congregation.

He said, "I want you to know we have a star in our midst." About that time, my friend who was sitting next to me, started shaking in silent laughter, turning red. I still didn't have a clue as to what was going on.

Then he said, "We would like her to come up and receive this gift from us."

Then he called my name and announced that I had formerly skated in the roller derby! Though under protest, I had no choice but to be a good sport, and went up to the front where he presented me with a gift-wrapped box of roller skates! We all roared with laughter as I graciously accepted the "gift."

The funnier thing was, when people had an opportunity to take me aside and inquire, they whispered, "Is it really true?"

The following Christmas, David's gift to me was a fabulous sketch he had drawn of Snoopy in his famous one-legged stance on skates, his scarf flowing behind him in the breeze, wearing a helmet that said "Big Ruth, der roller champ #1."

Throughout the years he took great delight in telling people how I used to skate in the derby. One would think the story would eventually fade away, but to my surprise and joy, for my last birthday my "sisters" presented me with a framed eight by ten actual photo of "my" roller derby team in action, with a picture of my laughing face superimposed on one of the gals in full uniform. It was autographed and looked very authentic. There was a lot of laughter and it brought back all the memories of how the story started. It is priceless!

From the time he was three or four, David wanted his own carpenter tool box and loved to use his hammer and nails. I used to fill up the trunk of our car with scraps of wood from the lumber yard and he would spend hours trying to build things. His love for working with wood grew into his full-time profession as a finish carpenter. He had quite a gift in his hands for drawing and was a true artist, which was also seen in the beautiful fireplace mantles and custom work he did for people. His other passion which started in childhood building model cars, grew into a love for street rods. He was in the process of building a street rod from an old Chevy pickup, which he never got the opportunity to finish.

He loved older people, little children, dogs, and cats, and had a special love for people who were developmentally or physically disabled. He had such a heart of compassion for those who were considered "not normal." I'm sure God gave him that compassion because of his own struggles. He got in trouble in Junior High School for defending a fellow student who was considered slow and "fun" to pick on. He fought the kid who was doing the bullying. He hated injustice done to those less fortunate. In growing up, David had a lot to overcome, within himself and in circumstances, but he was a fighter.

At the age of twelve he accepted Jesus as his Savior one summer at church camp. In spite of the struggles in life and his mistakes, he never stopped pressing toward God and becoming the man he was created to be. He did become that man. He always had a heart for God, and later in life chose to walk the high road with Him. He once told me some years ago that he didn't think there was any hope of healing for him this side of heaven, and all the while, unknown to himself, God was using him as an encourager in the lives of others, myself included. Whenever I was feeling down, the Lord would let him know, and I would get a phone call or a short visit that would lift my spirit, or he would say a prayer that always left me feeling lighter. In a conversation not long before his death, he told his biological father that its not important how you start life, but how you finish, that counts. David finished his race well.

He proudly served his country in the U.S. Air Force, and was a patriot at heart. The last time I visited him at his home in Emmett, he told me he didn't want to die there. I just thought it was because he always talked about wanting to live "over the hill," meaning up out of the valley and in the Boise area. God gave him the desire of his heart. He died "over the hill" at St. Al's hospital in Boise, and is buried at the beautiful veterans' cemetery there. His grave is directly under the beautiful American flag up on top of the hill overlooking the valley.

At his memorial service in our church, the place was packed out with people from all over the valley. It was truly a celebration of his life and the legacy of love he left behind. A friend of mine who attended said she had never been to any funeral like that one. She was amazed and said she was encouraged. It touched a lot of people. The sad part is that he was so well-loved and never knew it. May God help us to tell the people we love how much they mean to us and not take them for granted. In recent years David always ended his conversations with, "I love you," and "God bless your day." That was almost always the way we ended our conversations with each other.

His death was sudden and unexpected by us, although in looking back I'm sure he sensed it, and God in His goodness was trying to prepare me because two weeks before he died my heart was really burdened for him, seeing and hearing his weariness and exhaustion. You may not understand how I could view his death as God's gift to him, but it was, and to me as his mother, because my heart could take great comfort in the life he lived and the love he deposited here in the lives of all of us. It was a life that honored God. His death brought my other children back together in their relationships with each other and I'm sure impacted each of them deeply in different ways. I believe it also deepened their relationship with God. A wonderful thing about our God is that He uses everything and doesn't waste anything in the accomplishment of His purposes.

When I lived in Emmett some years ago, David sat out under the walnut tree in our front yard reading the Bible. His attention was drawn to Psalm 37:3-5 (NIV) which he shared with me and said he felt it was God's word to him that he should stay in Emmett and trust Him. I share them here with you:

"Trust in the Lord and do good; dwell in the land and enjoy safe pasture. Delight yourself in the Lord and he will give you the desires of your heart. Commit your way to the Lord; trust in him and he will do this: He will make your righteousness shine like the dawn, the justice of your cause like the noonday sun."

David became a source of joy and encouragement not only to myself, but to our family, and many others, as well. I look at his picture, and though I miss him terribly, the sorrow of not having him here is overruled by the joy and comfort of knowing he is indeed enjoying safe pasture at home with God, enjoying His fellowship, and being with loved ones who are there.

I'm comforted by the knowledge that even though he has moved on, he is still very much alive and well in heaven, and there will never be a disconnect from the love that so characterized and guided his life. That love connection is for eternity, and one day I will see him again, along with my husband, mother, father, grandparents, granddaughter, and niece. Some day there will be a real family reunion, when we are all in heaven. To God be the glory for all He has done!

Chapter 9

He Sets the Lonely in Families

After the loss of my son, David, in April of 2003, I was experiencing such depression, loneliness and fatigue, that my sister, Susan, flew up to Boise and helped me drive back to Sacramento for a much-needed time with family. It was a time of recovery with emotional and spiritual support where I wouldn't have to be alone. I also wanted to know if it were God's will for me to move back to California. The seven months there were so good for me. It was good to spend some time with my children and grandchildren, my brother, and sisters.

I lived with Susan, Dawny, and Lisa, all roommates, and we truly became family for each other. Susie and I have always been sisters, but we had never been given the opportunity to develop our relationship because of our age difference and circumstances. She was born late in our parents' lives and I was already grown with a family of my own so we didn't have time together as sisters usually do. In the last several years, due to her circumstances and mine, we were given the relationship we both had missed out on all our lives. I'm so thankful for my sis. She is a treasure!

Can you imagine four single women living in the same house, sharing two bathrooms, one kitchen, and living together in harmony? We did. It was truly a God thing—only He could bond us together and make the four of us sisters. That He did, and we ate together, laughed, cried, and prayed together and sometimes watched "chick flicks." We would look up songs online, and I would play the keyboard while we sang. We celebrated birthdays together, parties we'll never forget, with pictures to prove it. Those girls know how to party!

One birthday they gave me an African Dumbec drum and Lisa gave me lessons, so we drummed a little. It was exhilarating, and I do love that African beat! On my last birthday they even presented me with a family photo album of the four of us in various stages of celebration from the previous year. Dawny spent much time putting it together with her unique creativity. They then presented me with that gift of all gifts, the framed photograph of me with my roller derby team described in the preceding chapter. (A legend that will never die in my family, thanks to David.)

When I think of my time there with the girls and how God knew what each of us needed—a family—it causes me amazement and wonder at God's love for us. It's wonderful the way He sovereignly orchestrates the circumstances of our lives to bring us together with the people He knows we need to be with, who need us, and who will become family. Each of them has given something special to me, a gift of themselves in unselfish service. Susie, in truly making her home our home, with her unselfish generosity and helping hands, the morning cups of coffee she would bring to my room, and her prayers of encouragement. Lisa, and her funny words which I like to refer to as "Lisa-isms." She kept me laughing, giving time to help me with the computer, her encouragement, and her most recent hard work in designing the beautiful cover for this book. Dawny, and her wonderful creativity in the kitchen, her servant's heart in preparing meals which were delicious and sometimes surprising, with wonderful desserts. I am so thankful for my time there with them.

Even though the Lord has brought me back to Idaho, I know there will always be the bond of sisterhood between us. Wherever God takes us, that bond knows no distance. Our love and prayers are always with one another. I have never experienced anything like it before. He knew that each of us was hurting and in need of comfort. He brought together four individuals of different backgrounds and circumstances, with the common bond of loving the Lord, each of us needing a healing environment of love and support.

God created us to be in community with others, and within that community we can be healed if we're in an environment of love. Giving and receiving what each has to contribute to the well-being of the others is what love is all about. God in His wisdom knows what it takes to heal and grow us into the persons we were created to be.

The church family there was wonderful and spiritually vibrant, alive with the Holy Spirit and powerful life-giving messages. Each week was like receiving spiritual blood transfusions until I grew sufficiently strong and on the road to recovery again. A huge part of the recovery for me took place on Tuesday mornings at a gathering called Extreme Prayer which met at a lady's home there. Each week the ladies would love, encourage, and pray for me, and I would go away refreshed. It was in one of those meetings that they urged me to write this book. Those meetings combined with the services at church brought me a long way toward my healing.

However, I believe the greatest contributor to my recovery was the time spent with my three sisters, being embraced with unconditional love and acceptance, filling the need we all have to belong. We cannot heal alone. That's why His Word says in

Psalm 68:6 (NIV): *"He sets the lonely in families."* It is so true! I will forever thank Him for providing that family for me at such a critical time. He is so good!

Chapter 10

The Journey Home

The seven months in California were so good for me. During that time I wondered and prayed about the possibility of moving back to be with family. Though there was much healing there for me, several weeks before coming back home to Idaho, it was confirmed to me in several ways that God had work for me to do there, this book being one of His assignments.

Susan arranged to take some days off at the only time available to her, and so our date to come home was February 11th. The weather forecast was not good, with snow flurries predicted for the Sierras and throughout southern Idaho. As we prayed for guidance we both had peace about going ahead with our departure on the 11th. The day before, I packed up my room, loaded the car so everything was ready to go. The entire time we asked the Lord to make our path clear and let us know when we were to leave.

Early in the morning on the 11th, we checked the road conditions online and found chains were required on part of interstate I-80, so we waited. During the wait, I took another drive over to say a quick good-bye to my kids again. While on the way to their shop, a green car pulled up to a stop sign on the right of us and on the front license plate was one word in big letters—BOISE!

Lisa and I looked at each other and in unison we said, "Green means GO!"

After the good-bye hugs, we went back to the house and Susan checked the road conditions online once more. Sure enough, the chain requirement was lifted, so all things were clear for us to go, and we had peace about leaving then, even though storms were coming in all around us. We had complete peace, knowing God was leading us. Instead of fear, I felt exhilaration and joy about coming home.

The trip was a great example of how God's hand of protection is with us in the storms. It was awesome to see Him make a clear path for us all the way home. The only stretch of road that was wet and slushy was a short distance near Truckee. By the time we reached Reno the roads were dry and we had dry roads all the way home into my driveway. The exciting thing was to see the dark storms coming down all around us and yet the road we were on was dry, even though it was snowing! It's as though God had us in a tunnel! We were so in awe of His presence and protection.

When we reached Winnemucca, we stopped for a coffee break at an espresso shop and while there, my brother called, asking us where we were. I told him, and he said they were praying for us, informing me there had been a bad multi-car accident with two fatalities on I-80 just south of Truckee because of zero visibility, where we had been a couple of hours before. Another evidence of God's sovereign protection.

Earlier, I had been asking God to clear away the storms, but He was showing us something much greater—a powerful demonstration to let us see His hand of power and protection— by making a dry road *through* them. Sometimes, He doesn't clear away the storms, but takes us safely through. If one looked at the entire stormy area from a distance, to the physical eye there would be no way through, but God made the road safe and dry. Throughout the entire trip we sensed His presence, witnessed and received His protection and divine intervention, to get us safely to our destination.

Regardless of the weather forecast and seeing the storms on the weather channel, God guided us by several important factors that let us know His will and peace, and the green light to come home. He uses a combination of things to reveal His will in our lives, if we are seeking Him and are in tune with the desires of His heart and mind. I searched His Word which I lean on heavily for direction in finding His will.

The Scriptures He used to guide me were Psalm 32:8 (NIV), *"I will instruct you and teach you in the way you should go; I will counsel you and watch over you;"* also, Psalm 119:105 (NIV), *"Your Word is a lamp to my feet and a light for my path."* He then made it plain that He had work for me to do here in Idaho—people who needed me, and a book to write, which He kept bringing to my attention through other people, my own restlessness, and circumstances.

Then, He made time off from work available for my sister, which came sooner than my original thought of coming home on April 1st. And there was a growing and overwhelming desire in my heart to be back home in my house. In the midst of and undergirding all of these things, there was His peace. I also prayed Psalm 143:8,9 (NIV):

"Let the morning bring me word of your unfailing love, for I have put my trust in you. Show me the way I should go, for to you I lift up my soul."

In the NIV translation that phrase "cause me to know" is translated "show me the way I should go." I've learned not to make plans apart from Him, but always in prayer submit them to God's agenda and the wisdom of His Word, asking that He cause me to know and help me obey His will. Consequently, He worked in my heart and the circumstances to bring me home February 11, 2009. With a thankful heart I walked into my home and the new life He had in store for me.

Here I am reminded that He first must work His will into our hearts and wills before we can walk in His steps. Our God is so wise and tender with us when we have been crushed or suffered loss. He understands our pain and knows how much we need to be surrounded with loving arms and caring hearts. He so patiently loves us completely where we are and knows what we need—His healing balm applied to the broken places in our lives through those He sends to love us in our dark times. He loves us back to life and gently plants His desires in our hearts so we can walk with Him in this journey called life.

Our life with Him is truly a journey toward home.

Chapter 11

The Wine of New Life

January, 1994 my husband and I found ourselves at a place of major "burnout," both in his work in the nuclear industry, and in our marriage of 35 years. We were in Richland, Washington, where he worked at the nuclear power plant on the outskirts of town. It was at that point in our lives that we separated for a time.

Several months before I left, however, as I was reading my Bible one morning, the Lord had spoken to my heart through the first recorded miracle Jesus performed in His earthly ministry in which He turned water into wine at a wedding. God impressed upon my heart that He was going to "turn the water into wine" in our marriage, giving us a marriage we had never had in all of our 35 years together.

Little did I know what it would take to bring about that miracle, or that it would come as a result of my brokenness. God used my heartbreak to bring my husband to the realization of his great need for God and for me.

Later, in his own words he said, "He made me realize that I could no longer plunder through life without Him or without you."

Before leaving I prayed, asking God if I could go with His blessing, and was given peace to leave. A friend in Phoenix invited me to come and stay for awhile, so I gladly accepted the invitation to get away. I was treated like a queen in an environmen of love which was a balm of comfort and reassurance. I later saw how necessary it was for God to have my husband all to Himself without me in his life, in order to have a One-on-one encounter with him so his heart could be brought to a place of surrender and complete commitment to Him, and as a result, recommitment to me and our marriage.

I deeply honor his memory for the courage it took on his part to go before God on his knees, in honesty, humility, and repentance. During the separation he asked me to write to him everything I was feeling and say whatever needed to be said. So I did. Night after night I would wake up in tears, pour out my thoughts on a yellow legal-sized tablet, seal it up and mail it.

Not once did he ever accuse or criticize me of anything. He took full responsibility for our marriage, and when the writing was finished and he called me, his only response was, "I've got to change, that's all there is to it. I love you, and you belong here with me."

He asked me to come home then, and I remember so well how the feelings of hurt and betrayal welled up within me to the point that I wanted to yell into the phone, "No! I don't love you and I don't want to be married to you any more!"

I actually did say that to him at one point. I knew God was speaking to me to go home, even though I didn't want to. It was a struggle because I knew it was what God wanted, yet I was so wounded I just wanted out of the marriage, didn't want to be hurt any more by living in a loveless environment where I didn't matter and wasn't cherished. I couldn't do it any more.

God kept nudging me to go back, so I returned home, on Valentine's Day, no less. I came home to a changed man, one completely transformed by his encounter with God. Though my heart was still very much in a wounded state, when I stepped off the plane and saw him standing there waiting for me, looking so handsome, he had a new look about him, a peace and a glow that gave me peace and hope. I think that memory of him will always be in my heart.

The following June, we took a trip to Victoria, B.C. On our drive to Seattle, we stopped to tour the rain forest near the coast. As we were walking on the paths with the beautiful old trees on either side and a light mist falling, we came upon a giant old rotted tree that was fallen across our path. Along the full length of the old tree were new tiny trees growing up at the base of it. We stopped and took note of this scene in front of us, and it was a message of truth to our hearts, and a promise of new life for us. There was no one around us as we reflected upon it.

My husband said, "Isn't it amazing how new life can come out of death." We felt God's presence in that place and knew He was speaking to us of better things.

I wish it could be said that our marriage was instantly healed, but it wasn't. I came home in a very weakened and wounded condition. Before, I had been the strong one who prayed for and fought for our marriage. However, now it was my husband who had to be the strong one to fight for our marriage to be restored. We are required to forgive, which I did, but forgiveness doesn't heal our wounds. Our choice to forgive frees God's hand to begin the healing process in our hearts, which takes time.

Thankfully, from the day we reconciled, my husband never let a day go by without taking time to aggressively pray with me for my healing, our restoration, and blessing on our marriage. I use the word "aggressive" because it was his faithful determination to take responsibility for rebuilding our marriage through love and prayer, that our life together became the miracle God said it would be.

Our healing came as a result of his surrender to God and his commitment to take full responsibility for our restoration. The healing of my heart took about two years. I can in no way take credit for the miracle our marriage became, because had not my husband taken his God-given responsibility for us, we would not have remained together. I was simply obedient to the Lord in making myself available in the marriage for God to work His healing grace in both our hearts. It was truly a miracle of God's doing and I give Him all the praise and glory.

The last eleven years of our marriage were the miracle years for us, and I could not have asked for a more wonderful husband in the time that was left to us. He loved the Lord and me with all his heart and demonstrated that every day for the rest of his life. He became the wonderful man God created him to be. Not only did he pray daily for us, but also for our children and grand-children. He never ended a conversation with them on the phone without saying, "I love you."

And we never ended a day without saying, "I love you," to one another.

When he became ill with pulmonary fibrosis in 2001, and later had to be on oxygen 24/7, we drew closer to the Lord and each other. In the beginning when he was first diagnosed, I was in an emotional upheaval, a gamut of emotions and then denial because IPF is a fatal disease for which there is no cure. But as I was sitting with the Lord and my Bible one day, in my mind came this mental picture of my hands with a chokehold on Jim's throat, holding on to him for dear life.

Then I heard God say, "Release him to My perfect will and trust Me. He is not yours to keep."

In those moments I burst into tears and told the Lord I couldn't release him, that He would have to help me. In the mental scene before me, I imagined and felt God unclenching my fingers one by one until I could hold out to Him my empty hands. As I did, peace flooded my heart and I was okay. I knew the Lord was with us and everything was going to be okay, that our lives and times were in His hands—and above all, He is trustworthy and faithful.

My prayer was for God's perfect healing and that He would be glorified in every aspect of what we were going through.

We began and ended each day in prayer, went for drives to enjoy the beauty of God's creation, took time to notice the morning sunrises and evening sunsets. Sometimes he would step out on the front porch and ask me to join him there to view the beautiful sunset. There were many mornings when we would sit out on our patio enjoying our coffee, listening to the birds, and watching the funny antics of the squirrels at play on the lawn and in the trees.

It's amazing how priorities change when a sudden, life-changing crisis is dropped into your life, an unexpected event that redirects your thinking and helps you establish new priorities of what's really important. It changes our perspective and causes us to take time to enjoy the simple blessings found in the gift of each day, more aware than ever of the importance of living in the present moment.

The more we enjoyed the beauty of God's creation, the more we became aware and comforted by the knowledge that He is still on the throne and in control of our lives. During the several years before his passing, when anyone would call and ask him how he was doing, his response was always, "Just fine." I know there were days when he didn't feel so good, but he would never let me hear him say anything that would cause me to be concerned for him. I'm sure it was God's keeping grace and sustaining strength, because he always looked so good, well-dressed and handsome, that when he died, people were shocked.

God kept him strong until the morning of the day He took him home. That was the only day he didn't have the strength to shower, shave and dress himself. We took communion together that morning. He asked me to pray and said he would agree with me. I knelt beside his chair, held hands and prayed. Our prayer that morning was that God would reach down His hand and bring complete healing to him and we thanked Him for His faithfulness, love and grace. I felt tears of release for him as I prayed.

Less than two hours later, he was shaking and cold. I covered him with a blanket, called our son David who came, and called for an ambulance.

Life Flight arrived, and he was wheeled out on the gurney. At the doorway of the helicopter, I put my arms around him, kissed him, laid my head on his chest. In three easy breaths he went from breathing earth's air to breathing the celestial air of heaven. He left us on October 21, 2005, one day before my birthday and two days before his. He would have been 70.

Shortly after that when at home sitting in Jim's recliner, I thought to myself, "Lord, You really did "life flight" him home, didn't You?"

Regarding our marriage and the miracle God performed, it could not have taken place had we not been willing and committed to stay in the marriage to cooperate with Him in the making of that miracle, which was only by the work of His grace. I thank Him for His patience and His radical love that pursues us, His grace and unfathomable commitment to love us without reservation until we are made whole in Him. Some are healed on earth and some are healed only in heaven. Praise be to Him for His faithfulness to honor His Word and our faith.

When it comes to miracles, generally people tend to think in terms of raising someone from the dead, blind eyes opened, a physical healing. But I believe the greatest miracle is that moment when God encounters and invades a human heart to meet and transform a heart to become one with Him in His desires, His dream and purpose for a life. He empowers us to love people as He loves the people in our lives.

In studying the miracles in the Bible, I've found that in nearly every case, Jesus required the participation of the people involved. At the miracle of turning the water into wine, recorded in the second chapter of John, Jesus required the servants to fill the water pots and do what He asked of them.

In the miracle of feeding the five thousand in the book of Matthew, a boy gave his small lunch of bread and fish which Jesus blessed, broke, and multiplied into an abundance which fed the multitude. He required the disciples to distribute the multiplied bread and fish to the crowd. When He raised Lazarus from the dead, He instructed the disciples to unwrap the grave clothes and let him go. When He healed the man with the withered hand, He instructed the man to *"reach forth your hand."*

He could have performed any one of those miracles with just a word, but He didn't. He required them to participate with Him in those miracles. He does the miracles, but most of the time requires us to be willing participants in order to receive the miracle He has in mind, the intention of His heart. Indeed, God does the miracles, but He has chosen us to be involved in delivering them. Through our willingness to be obedient to Him, we are privileged to become a witness and recipient of His miracles for our greater happiness and His greater glory.

Chapter 12

Ðo You Want to Get Weℓℓ?

"Do you want to get well?"

This was the question Jesus asked the crippled man when He found him lying at the the pool. We find it recorded in John 5:1-15 (NIV). The man had been in his crippled condition for thirty-eight years when Jesus approached him with the question. Here is his story:

Its setting is in Jerusalem at a pool called Bethesda where many disabled people used to lie, the blind, lame and paralyzed, in the hope of being healed. The Hebrew meaning of the word Bethesda literally means "Place of Outpouring" or "House of Grace." The sick gathered or were carried there because periodically the waters would be stirred up, and the first person to get into the water after the stirring would be healed of whatever sickness he had. Some scholars suggest that the stirring was caused by an intermittent spring, and the NKJV v. 4 states that an angel went down and stirred the waters.

Irrespective of the source of the waters being stirred, the evidence of God's supernatural healing grace and power were present. The man to whom Jesus addressed his question had been an invalid for so many years, something within the man prompted Jesus to ask him the question:

"When Jesus saw him lying there and learned that he had been in this condition for a long time, he asked him, 'Do you want to get well?' 'Sir,' the invalid replied, 'I have no one to help me into the pool when the water is stirred. While I am trying to get in, someone else goes down ahead of me.' Then Jesus said to him, 'Get up! Pick up your mat and walk.' At once the man was cured; he picked up his mat and walked...Later Jesus found him at the temple and said to him, 'See, you are well again. Stop sinning or something worse may happen to you.'"

As I was thinking about the subject of healing and all that is involved in a person being made well, Jesus' healing of the man at the pool came to mind, and so I studied the Scriptures to gain insight from them. The reason I chose the above question as the title for this chapter is because it is so relevant to the life of every individual who has ever desired to be well in spirit, soul, and body. There is much for us to learn from this incident in the life of the man and the ministry of Jesus as He went about healing the sick.

I believe He wants us well and still asks the question today as He seeks us out in our individual conditions from which we need healing. This is not to say that all physical sickness is sin related. However, in the case related above, it was. Research has proven that negative, destructive attitudes of the mind and heart affect the entire spirit, soul, and body, and do cause disease.

It is not only true that sin causes disease, but it is also true that when a heart has been broken and a human spirit crushed by the cruelty and sins of others, it creates trauma from which is difficult to recover and results in deep wounding of the spirit. It can result in a deep-seated anger and bitterness of soul if the person doesn't turn to God for the help and healing through a love relationship with Himself through His Son. He is the beginning place and the source of our healing and restoration. It is as the Scriptures tell us in Proverbs 18:14 (NIV): *"A man's spirit sustains him in sickness, but a crushed spirit who can bear?"*

I don't believe any person in this condition can find healing on their own, but *if* there is an earnest desire to be healed and restored, with a willingness to seek God, Who alone is the source of our healing and hope, He will hear the desperate cry of the broken and send the help He knows is needed. He honors desperate prayers. He truly is our Healer and Great Physician, and there is no hurt so deep that His love and grace cannot reach to touch, heal, and restore.

As I write this, my thoughts are drawn to the many children who are abused physically, mentally, and sexually who have been traumatized, used for self-gratification and greed, then rejected, abandoned, and thrown away by those they should have been able to trust. If they live long enough, they grow up to be bruised, broken people who so desperately need the healing love of our God Who is their only refuge and place of hope. My heart wants to wrap my arms around them and bring them to the One Who loves and values them and wants to heal their deepest wounds.

In Proverbs 14:30 (NIV) we read: *"A heart at peace gives life to the body, but envy rots the bones."*

"Pleasant words are a honeycomb, sweet to the soul and healing to the bones." Proverbs 16:24 (NIV)

"A cheerful heart is good medicine, but a crushed spirit dries up the bones." Proverbs 17:22 (NIV)

Ps. 34:14 (NIV) gives us this promise and hope: *"The Lord is close to the brokenhearted and saves those who are crushed in spirit."*

Also, we see in Ps. 61:1,2 (NKJV) the psalmist's prayer, which can be ours when our hearts are overwhelmed: *"Hear my cry,*

O God; attend to my prayer...I will cry to You when my heart is overwhelmed; lead me to the rock that is higher than I."

Jesus said of Himself in Isaiah 61:1-3 (NIV) that He is the Healer of broken hearts:

"He has sent Me to bind up the brokenhearted, to proclaim freedom to the captives and release from darkness for the prisoners, to comfort all who mourn, to bestow on them a crown of beauty instead of ashes, the oil of gladness instead of mourning, and a garment of praise instead of a spirit of despair."

And a verse which has spoken to my own heart many times over the years is Proverbs 13:12 (NKJV): *"Hope deferred makes the heart sick, but when the desire comes, it is a tree of life."*

We live in a fallen world and have an enemy whose name is satan, whose aim it is to steal, kill and destroy lives. We read in Genesis how he succeeded in deceiving Adam and Eve, convincing them that the fruit God commanded them not to eat would make them wise like God Himself. And so, they ate, their choice causing their relationship with God to be broken, and not only theirs but all mankind's as well.

I don't think it's possible to comprehend the full magnitude of how far and deep was the fall of mankind and all creation with it because of their choices. Choices. How far reaching they are! Like a pebble thrown into a pond, it causes a ripple effect that reaches far beyond its point of impact. It brings me to tears when I think of the terrible ramifications selfish choices have on God's heart, and the grief it must have caused Him to see the objects of His affection, His highest creation made in His own image, dishonor Him by disobeying His only commandment— do not eat of one fruit.

Satan thought he had won, but he is the world's biggest liar and loser; for the great good news is that God had a plan to redeem mankind from the curse, knowing full well what Adam's and Eve's choice would be. His plan, His remedy, even then, was and still is the Savior of the world, Jesus Christ His Son!

Because the results of our choices are so far reaching, I believe the Lord has prompted me to address the condition which affects all of us and which concerns Him most—our heart conditions, those issues we all have to one degree or another, as in the case of the man in our story. It's obvious from Jesus' question and the statement He made to the man after his healing, that he had sin issues which always originate in the heart. Jesus went right to the heart of the matter when He asked him if he wanted to get well. The excuses he made were evidence of a deeper issue.

We all have issues of the heart which we need to face, and be healed from, especially when Jesus confronts us with the same question, "Do you *want* to get well?"

It's a question that only you and He can answer.

As for me, my heart's response to Him is "Yes, Lord! I want to get well!"

What does your heart desire?

As many Scriptures indicate to us, there seems to be a direct connection between the health of the soul and the health of the body. I believe the biggest roadblock to healing is unforgiveness, the refusal to forgive an offense and release the offender from your personal judgment. I recently heard a definition of unforgiveness as being when you drink poison and hope the other person dies from it.

When unforgiveness continues to be harbored in the heart, it produces a root of bitterness which spreads like a cancer, affecting not only your life, but all relationships with the people your life touches and influences. It will destroy all of your relationships, including your health, and is like a brick wall which literally prevents you from moving forward or making progress. You cannot tunnel under it, go around or over it, because it is a barrier that can only be removed through forgiveness which must be from your heart.

Sometimes the person hardest to forgive is yourself, but it is vitally necessary if you want peace and healing. The Scripture in I John 1:9 (NKJV) states: *"If we confess our sins, He is faithful and just to forgive us our sins and to cleanse us from all unrighteousness."*

That means we need to believe it and act on it. Unwillingness to forgive yourself is a slap in the face to God's integrity and truth, for He is Truth and can speak nothing less. If you do not forgive yourself it is the same as calling God a liar because you refuse to believe His Word is true and receive it. If you want to know His peace, it will require faith, humility, honesty, and a decision of your will. It requires mentally bringing every offense and the offender to the cross and asking God from the heart to fill you with His grace to forgive them (including yourself), then choosing to do so.

Though forgiveness is a choice, healing is a process that requires time. Forgiveness doesn't heal the wound, but sets the healing process in motion, so once you've chosen to forgive, God's hand is free to pour His healing grace and love into the wound to bring wholeness, restoration, and peace. There are no options if you want to be well. If you are unwilling to forgive, then neither will God forgive you, and the memories of those unforgiven offenses against you (or ones you have committed) will torment you for the rest of your life.

Unforgiveness literally binds you to the offense and makes it impossible for you to see or love the person as God desires. Jesus' words to us from Mark 11:25,26 (NKJV) are:

"And whenever you stand praying, if you have anything against anyone, forgive him, that your Father in heaven may also forgive you your trespasses. But if you do not forgive, neither will your Father in heaven forgive your trespasses."

Let's look again at the dialogue between Jesus and the crippled man in our Scripture reference. When Jesus asked him the question, one would have thought the man's answer would have been a resounding, "Yes!" but not so. The man responded with excuses as to why he had been in that condition for so long.

When Jesus ordered the man to *"Get up! Pick up your mat and walk,"* Jesus cut through his excuses and in His mercy healed the man. Jesus commanded him to pick up his mat, which represented the bed of excuses he had been lying on for so long, along with his passive and half-hearted attitude. He healed him and left him with no excuses.

I see in this that if you want to be healed, it requires action on your part, whatever the step is that you need to take toward your healing. When Jesus died on the cross, He provided everything you need in order to be healed and walk in wholeness. When you humble yourself before Him in honesty and ask Him the right question, you can always count on Him to speak the truth about whatever condition you're in, and the forward steps you need to take to become whole. Holding on to past offenses paralyzes and cripples you. Reaching to take Jesus' hand in humility, honesty, and the desire to be healed are steps forward toward healing.

Whatever your need is in the realm of healing, whether it is spiritual, emotional, mental, or physical, it takes courage to walk toward wholeness, and sometimes will involve pain in the process. We have to be willing to go through pain to get out of pain, just as in physical therapy it is painful to do the very exercises that will strengthen and heal you. When past hurtful incidents are remembered and your heart has determined to forgive and be healed of the past, there is pain that is actually bringing healing to the memory, and once it is healed the pain is gone forever. When I think of the healing forgiveness brings, I like to use the analogy of a bee without a stinger. When true healing from a wound is complete, a person may have a flash-back of a memory, but it has lost its sting and has no more power to hurt you; there is no more pain in it.

It is sad, but true, that there are people who don't want to deal with their issues and are more comfortable living in the pain of their crippled or dysfunctional condition, whatever kind it may be. It takes courage to admit when you're wrong and need help, but *realizing, desiring, and seeking* it is a beginning and a huge step forward.

Sometimes a person who has been traumatized comes to the point in life where he or she needs professional assistance to work through very difficult things. When we reach the point of "God, I can't do this anymore, please help me!" He has help waiting for us. None of us can heal by ourselves. It takes helping, caring hearts in an environment of love to help us heal, and I'm thankful for the many professional counseling and prayer ministries that are available.

At one point in my life, I sought the help of a Christian counselor for a few months after the loss of my son. God used her in a wonderful way to help, comfort, and encourage me with practical steps I could take to move forward. Though God does provide support and help through others, He does not want us to ever become co-dependent on them. He alone is our Healer, but uses others as coaches and encouragers with words of wisdom and counsel to help us grow in our walk with Him. A good counselor will never desire you to look only to them, but will always encourage you to seek and depend upon God.

Though I've appreciated, received, and grown from the good counsel I've received from others, I have found the greatest counselor is the Word of God and the greatest Psychologist is Jesus our Healer and Great Physician. The realization of His love for me and the awareness of His Presence is my greatest comfort and joy. In Scripture some of His names are *Wonderful Counselor, Mighty God, Everlasting Father, Prince of Peace*. He hears the cries of the broken hearted and sets captives free. If we draw near to Him, He will draw near to us. God has a pathway of healing for each of us, which begins and ends in Him.

Many places in Scripture confirm the truth that Christ's atoning work on the cross provided not only salvation for our souls; but also healing for our bodies. Isaiah 53:4,5 (NKJV),

Matt. 8:16,17 (NKJV), and others. I have experienced His healing touch in my body on many occasions and believe His healing miracles are for today. I believe that He empowers Christians with His Holy Spirit to lay hands on the sick and see them recover. He is doing this in many places throughout the world; and I've also been privileged to be used in this way on several occasions, to Him be the glory. Jesus Christ is the same yesterday, today and forever, and His healing power hasn't changed or diminished from the time He established the Church on the Day of Pentecost when He poured out His Holy Spirit on the apostles and those gathered together with them.

The gifts of the Holy Spirit that Jesus poured out on His Church were for the purpose of revealing the living Lord Jesus Christ and His power to save to the uttermost those who call on Him, to bring a harvest of many souls into His kingdom, for His honor and glory. None of the gifts are about us, but about Him, to bring others to Him. Unfortunately, there are some churches today who mistakenly believe that the power of the Holy Spirit to operate in His healing gifts, and other gifts, are no longer valid today. Consequently, those churches who embrace that theology are without the power of the Holy Spirit, and are powerless to bring healing and deliverance to those who are so in need of both.

I share the following story to simply show that God can and will use anyone who is yielded to Him, listening, and obedient to His Spirit's leading. He can use the weakest of us if we're willing to say *yes* to Him. Our educational background and training, or lack thereof, has no bearing on His ability to use us for His glory to benefit others. He wants to provide for the needs of those He loves, and allows us the privilege of participating with Him to accomplish it. Miracles are always to reveal the greatness of God and to demonstrate His compassion and desire for relationship with us.

On one occasion, many years ago, I flew to California to be with my parents when my dad was sick with throat cancer. He had been a heavy smoker for many years. The doctors had given him radiation treatments but the cancer was still spreading. As I was asleep, the Lord spoke a Scripture to my mind from James 5:14-16 several times throughout the night and said if we would anoint dad with oil and pray for him, he would be healed. The Scripture in James says that if anyone is sick let him call for the elders and anoint him with oil, praying in faith, and he will be healed.

The church my mom attended didn't believe in anointing with oil, but I knew what God had said, so I told Mom and my brother what I knew the Lord was telling us to do. I told Dad that the Lord wanted to heal him, and he reluctantly agreed to let us do this for him, not believing at all that it would make any difference. He told me later he just did it to "get me off his back." My brother came over, and we had dad sit in a chair, as we anointed his head with oil, and prayed the prayer of faith.

Simply put, the Lord healed him just as He said He would. God is so faithful, if we will just learn to listen, believe and obey! Shortly after that, he went back to the doctors, and when the panel of specialists examined him, they found no trace of cancer. The doctors were amazed and couldn't explain it, but Mom didn't have any trouble at all telling them exactly how Dad was healed! Did it make a believer out of him? Absolutely! To God be the glory for the great things He has done! God still operates today all over the world through His disciples who will simply believe, listen, and obey.

As much as I strongly believe in, have received, witnessed, and participated in some miraculous healings, I know God is sovereign in His ways and His ways are higher than ours, beyond our understanding. Only He holds the answers to why He doesn't always heal someone physically. Sometimes He heals them here on earth, and sometimes He heals them by taking them through death for reasons of His own.

I believe God sometimes bypasses physical healing, perhaps because He is aiming to accomplish something much deeper in the hearts of the family members (and others) of the loved ones who are taken, such as strengthening character and deepening trust in Him regardless of circumstances. Sometimes He breaks into the busyness and skewed priorities in life to remind us of what our number one priority should be, a right relationship with our Creator and loving the people He places in our lives.

My son David died three days after suffering a stroke. At this writing, it has been two years and two and a half months since April 15, 2008. It was such a shock to all of us, and many prayers went up for his recovery. At one point he rallied and responded so well to everyone present with recovery of speech and movement of his left side, the doctor, nurses, and his family felt we would have a miracle and see him recover.

However, God had other plans for Dave, and at 1:55 a.m. Tuesday morning, April 15, 2008, his spirit left and he went home to God. He had been in perfect health, would have turned 54 on his birthday which would have been July 18. My heart in shock, I breathed a prayer asking God for some kind of comfort; would He help me understand? Several days later, I received a card in the mail with a Scripture from Isaiah 57:1,2 (NIV) and as I read it, I cried, and said, "Thank You" to God for the comfort it gave. David was a Christian who loved the Lord and the people in his life. His life was a demonstration of love wherever he went. The words of Isaiah were God's message to my heart regarding His reason for taking Dave home to be with Him. The words speak for themselves:

"The righteous perish, and no one ponders it in his heart; devout men are taken away, and no one understands that the righteous are taken away to be spared from evil. Those who walk uprightly enter into peace; they find rest as they lie in death."

God sees the road ahead and I believe as He looks at His children and sees their weariness and how much they can endure, sometimes makes the decision to call them home.

On October 21, 2005, my husband Jimmy passed away and went home to heaven two days before his 70th birthday after a four-year battle with pulmonary fibrosis. Though I prayed earnestly and believed with all my heart he would be healed, God had spoken to my heart to trust Him and release Jim to Him because he belonged to Him. Those four years were years of real living and seizing the moments, enjoying what really mattered—relationship with God and each other. God did heal him perfectly, by taking him home. He was to be life-flighted to St. Al's Hospital in Boise, but as he was at the door of the helicopter, he breathed three easy breaths and was gone.

I thought I was prepared to say good-bye and release him, but I wasn't, so I couldn't bring myself to say it.

I just said, "I love you."

It was bitter-sweet, because even though pulmonary fibrosis is an incurable and fatal disease, God did shower His strengthening grace on my husband. He was strong up until the day he died, which is highly unusual since most PF patients are bedfast for the last few months of their lives. He was always dressed, showered and shaved and looked so good; he didn't look sick, except the last few days when you could see his tiredness. People were shocked to learn that he had died. But we had been given extended time together, more than the doctors thought possible, and one of our pastors said watching us go through his sickness had impacted their lives and strengthened their faith. God was so good to us in giving us that extra time, and we were blessed that it was good time. It's true that He makes *all* things work together for our good and His glory.

On March 23, 1999, our granddaughter, Samantha, went home to heaven after she had suffered with pneumonia and a genetic seizure disorder from birth which left her incapacitated, legally blind, and unable to walk, talk, or function. So many prayers had gone up for her healing, and with much faith. Cindy, Sami's mom, our entire family and friends, all sent up many prayers, but God in His mercy saw what she needed. Though she was incapacitated, she loved to be held and talked to, could laugh, and had such a beautiful smile. We were blessed with her for much longer than the doctors said was possible. She completed seven years and six months, and would have been eight the following September 26th.

I believe it is always with God's mercy when the life of one of His children is taken. I trust Him to do only and always what is best for me and my children who were dedicated and given to Him a long time ago. Heaven is a very real place, and my heart rests in the faith that one day I will see not only Dave, and Jim and Sami, but my other loved ones who are there, as well. God's ways are higher than our ways, and I trust Him and His ways, even though I don't always understand His "why's."

You hold in your hand the key to your emotional and spiritual healing. That key is the door of your heart which only you can open by your desire and your choice. God's desire for each of us is that we would choose forgiveness and healing, life and blessing. As previously shared, He longs to give us that in a personal relationship with Him through the provision and sacrifice of His Son Jesus Christ. He longs to see us embrace the life and destiny He has planned for us through our willingness to say "yes" to Him, and to commit our lives to loving and obeying Him.

Life is full of many injustices. There are many abuses in every aspect of society; in marriages and families, in government at any level, in the church, in the corporate world between employers and employees, in the educational system and every other institution, because we live in a fallen world. And the world isn't getting any better, but darker and more corrupt as the days go by. All we are seeing in the corruption, chaos and disasters around us are signs according to Bible prophecy that we are living in the last days before Christ returns for His Church.

The world's condition is all the more reason for us to look up to the One Who alone has all authority over life and will settle all accounts, Who will bring justice where there has been injustice and right the wrongs. Acts 17:30,31 (NKJV) speaks to us these words calling us to repentance:

"Truly, these times of ignorance God overlooked, but now

commands all men everywhere to repent, because He has appointed a day on which He will judge the world in righteousness by the Man whom He has ordained. He has given assurance of this to all by raising Him from the dead."

Also, from Acts 3:19 (NKJV):

"Repent therefore, and be converted, that your sins may be blotted out, so that times of refreshing may come from the presence of the Lord."

Since we cannot escape the injustices and abuses in life, the one and only way those things can be used to bring something good from them which will bring honor to God, is our willingness to forgive the offenders, committing the offenses and abuses into God's hands Who alone has the ability to heal us, then asking forgiveness of others where we have offended. Letting go of the offense is humanly impossible without His grace and help, for we are not humanly capable of healing our own heart and soul. But if we ask God the Holy Spirit to fill our hearts with the grace of His forgiveness, we can trust Him to do in us what we cannot do for ourselves. This is the key to our healing and freedom which will open the door and enable us to move forward to fulfill God's purpose for our life, and the dream which He placed in our hearts long ago.

When Jesus was on the cross, He said, *"Father, forgive them for they know not what they do."*

The abuses and cruelty committed against Him were far greater than anything you or I will ever have to endure. Yet, if we truly determine to be His disciple, we will be called upon in life to identify with Him in His sufferings, and to walk with Him in situations where we will be rejected and misunderstood for His name's sake. His aim is to develop and perfect His love within us, and to create in us unoffendable hearts. To become like His Son is the Father's heart for us so we may be brought into all that He has planned for us in order to fulfill our destiny and His purpose.

For God to achieve this victory in us, we must forgive from

our hearts those who have wounded, abused, or maligned us. If you set your heart to forgive your offenders and offenses, He will heal and set you free to love as He loves, and fulfill all that He has purposed in His heart to accomplish for and through you for His glory.

In reading over this chapter, I've wondered if it's too repetitive. After asking the Lord how He sees it, I've come to the peaceful conclusion to leave it as is. I'm reminded of how many times the Scriptures are repetitive in their exhortation to love and forgive. So, I leave with you His words to us from John 8:36 (NKJV) which are:

"Therefore if the Son makes you free, you shall be free indeed."

Chapter 13

Run Toward the Vision

In recent weeks I've been asking the Lord to motivate and strengthen me to be consistent in taking daily walks and to help me in the stewardship of my health. Many is the night that I've asked Him to give me a vision that would create a desire for walking, and have asked Him to command new strength for my body. Walking is one of the best ways to regain strength and build endurance, but I've not had the inner motivation or energy until several weeks ago. I know the Lord has a plan and a future for me, and part of it will require my best physical condition.

After my prayer one night, during my sleep a vivid picture was planted in my mind. It was a picture of myself in a white track uniform with a number five on the jersey. (Number five is my number, the one God gave me after a series of events led me to study its meaning—it means God's grace, but that is another story in itself!) I was wearing running shoes.

I heard Him say, "Run toward the vision."

When I awakened, all I could see was me in a track uniform, number five, running shoes, ready to run. The thought occurred that the picture of me in a track uniform with the number five was God's way of saying that by His grace I will finish my race. He was also showing me that I needed to stay in the race, and run it with the heart to win, not grow weary or lose the desire to go on to the finish. In essence, He was giving me a renewed vision of what He can do if I will get up and move my feet in step with Him, trusting in Him to strengthen me.

Every day since then and throughout the day, that mental picture is so clear and strong it is as though it's glued to my forehead. I can truly say it has certainly motivated me! I bought some good walking shoes, and have begun walking, beginning with a mile interspersing one-minute jogs in between. Then I increased it to a mile and a half. The first few days after the walks, my bones felt like they weren't going to cooperate and I wasn't sure I could continue like that.

Since moderation has never been one of my virtues, it seemed to me if one mile would be good for me, then two miles should give me twice the benefit! After a couple of weeks of the walk/jog routine, my ankles hurt and began to swell, which forced me to take a two-week leave of absence from the walks to give my ankles a rest, and hopefully gain some wisdom about overdoing. Starting over, I kept the exercise to a brisk walk, deciding to leave the jogging to the younger generation.

I've discovered that to "run toward the vision" really means to run spiritually toward the goal of becoming like Christ and all He created me to be. It means to continue moving forward into life and not looking back at what is past. I'm pleased to say I've seen an improvement in my stamina level as I've determined to be disciplined and continue walking, and my body is responding with new strength. The best part is, I feel so good to be doing it, knowing I'm getting stronger each day, and pleasing the Lord in what He is calling me to do. My spirit is exhilarated with expectancy for what God has in mind for my future. I don't know what that will look like, but I'm sure His plan includes many things I never thought or dreamed I would be doing. Though it is late in life and my attempt at jogging has slowed to a brisk walk, on the inside I'm running the race He has set before me, and am determined to keep walking, remembering it is never too late for God to do abundantly above all my expectations, for He is a God of miracles! God often waits and saves His best for last. I know not what my future holds, but I know the One Who holds my future!

I hadn't planned to include this story in the book until I felt the prompting to write about it today, so there is a purpose in sharing it with you. Whatever God does in our lives He uses to encourage others. I believe He has a vision for every one of us, and His best is yet to be. However, His greatest vision is that we would know Him and Jesus Christ Whom He sent, be filled with His Spirit, and become a reflection of His love and life as a light in the darkness of this world.

Throughout the history recorded in the Bible, God has spoken or revealed His directions to His people in dreams and visions, and He still does today. God's Word has been given to us to instruct and show us His ways and it is the final authority on which everything is to be judged. Dreams and visions which are from Him are always in alignment with the truth and wisdom of His Word, which He will use to confirm what He has already spoken to us from the Scriptures. They are given to encourage, inspire and build our faith.

Any dream or vision should always be examined in the light of God's Word, for there are many dreams and visions which are not from God, but could be from other sources such as yourself, or from the evil one. Our lives should never be built upon dreams or visions themselves, but on the only foundation upon which we can safely build—the Lord Jesus Christ and His Word.

I Corinthians 3:11 (NIV) speaks to us:

"For no one can lay any foundation other than the one already laid, which is Jesus Christ."

Before the picture was planted in my mind of me in a track suit and running shoes, I had been reading and studying I Corinthians 9:24-27, which is a description of one competing in a race. Also, I had been reading and thinking about the words of Hebrews 11 and 12; their meaning makes it quite clear that our journey with Christ is a race to be run, and a race to be won. I love the verses in Hebrews 12:1-2 (NKJV):

"Therefore we also, since we are surrounded by so great a cloud of witnesses, let us lay aside every weight, and the sin which so easily ensnares us, and let us run with endurance the race that is set before us, looking unto Jesus, the author and finisher of our faith, who for the joy that was set before Him endured the cross, despising the shame, and has sat down at the right hand of the throne of God."

And Hebrews 12:3 (NIV):

"Consider him who endured such opposition from sinful men, so that you will not grow weary and lose heart."

When Jesus taught His disciples He often used parables, (short stories) to give them mental pictures of earthly scenes as a comparison to explain spiritual truths. In several of the parables He introduced them with the statement:

"The kingdom of heaven is like..."

Then He would tell the story, painting for them word pictures of the earthly scene to help them understand the spiritual meaning.

I believe every invention ever created and every dream ever fulfilled for the betterment of mankind began as a picture in someone's mind before it ever became a reality—vision that motivated and energized the person to keep on working toward that which he was passionate about, and seeing it become a reality. It brings to mind also the fact that many who have achieved great things had times of failure in their attempts. Yet they learned through their mistakes and never gave up; through determination and perseverance they became successful inventors, entrepreneurs, statesmen, missionaries, preachers, teachers, authors, etc., doing what they were created to do, all because of vision—the way God created each of us—with design.

There is that special something for which you were created and which He wants to fulfill through you on this earth. You have only to believe and ask.

Jeremiah 29:11-13 (NIV) expresses God's heart to you:

"'For I know the plans I have for you', declares the Lord, 'plans to prosper you and not to harm you, plans to give you hope and a future. Then you will call upon me and come and pray to me, and I will listen to you. You will seek me and find me when you seek me with all your heart.'"

My hope for you is that God will use this book to help you catch a glimpse of His heart, His vision, His dream for your life and stir you to pursue Him with all your heart.

I've waited many years for the fulfillment of God's dream for my life. I've found that when God gives a vision, there is a process that takes place in which there is death to that vision, experientially, circumstantially, and spiritually. It will cause you to wonder if God really gave it to you in the first place, or if it was just your own. I've learned to trust Him more deeply, and also what it is to enjoy and cherish His presence each day. My hope is that He will find me faithful in loving Him and the people He has placed in my life.

I've learned in all He takes me through His greatest aim is to teach me to love as He loves, and to be transformed in character to become like His Son. During the death years of a vision, He develops and matures us through many trials. He tests our faith, and us. He wants to find us faithful. If we are faithful with what He gives us to walk in, living worthy of His trust, He will use our circumstances to build a platform from which we will be qualified to minister His love, life and encouragement to others.

God brings death to every vision He gives, so that when He brings it to birth and resurrects it, no one but Him will get the glory because it will be nothing less than a miracle of His doing. No person will be able to say, "Look what I've done." Only He can bring life out of death. Only He can make a miracle from an impossibility. He does, and He will!

I think about the place to which God has brought me, of new life and purpose, strength and energy. I believe His dream for me is to invest my life, love and prayers to help someone else fulfill God's purpose and calling for their life, thus fulfilling His dream and vision for them and myself as well. There would be no greater joy for me!

In this race of life, many is the time over the years when in exhaustion I would read Isaiah 40:28-31 (NKJV) and know that only as God strengthened me could I go on. Now, after so long, by His grace I am experiencing the reality of the promise in these Scriptures:

"Do you not know? Have you not heard? The Lord is the everlasting God, the Creator of the ends of the earth. He will not grow tired or weary, and his understanding no one can fathom. He gives strength to the weary and increases the power of the weak. Even youths grow tired and weary, and young men stumble and fall; but those who hope in the Lord will renew their strength. They will soar on wings like eagles; they will run and not grow weary, they will walk and not be faint."

If you are in need of a fresh renewal of life, hope and strength, God is there for you and invites you to come to Him and ask.

After all these years, I find that Jesus is truly my vision Who grows brighter in my heart every day. His presence is my greatest joy, and pleasing Him is my goal and my reward. Each day my desire is to run with my eyes fixed on Him who is the author and finisher of my faith, until one day I will cross the finish line, and run straight into His arms!

Chapter 14

The Power of His Name

There is no sweeter or more powerful name than the Name of Jesus. His name means Savior. In Matthew 1:21 (NKJV) speaking of Mary, the angel tells Joseph: *"And she will bring forth a Son and you shall call His name Jesus, for He will save His people from their sins."* And Philippians 2:9-11 (NKJV) *"Therefore God also has highly exalted Him and given Him the name which is above every name, that at the name of Jesus every knee should bow, of those in heaven, and of those on earth, and of those under the earth, and that every tongue should confess that Jesus Christ is Lord, to the glory of God the Father."*

Oh, that wonderful name! JESUS. Just the mention of His Name thrills my heart and brings the sweet assurance and awareness of His presence with me at *all* times, in *all* situations.

All power and authority belong to Him. In Luke 10:19, Jesus gave His disciples power and authority over the works of the enemy. Today, if you are a Christian, you can have the confidence that through the power of the Holy Spirit, Who indwells every Christian, He still gives His disciples authority over the evil one and the forces of darkness when we are forced into dangerous circumstances.

As our Creator, He longs for us to understand and realize Whose we are and that we carry within us the very Spirit and Life of the One Who created not only us, but all of creation. He wants us to walk with Him in the assurance that not only does He indwell us, He empowers us to confront and overcome evil when we are faced with it.

The authority He vested in His early disciples hasn't diminished, nor has He changed His mind or His intentions that His Church be filled and empowered with the Holy Spirit. He wants us to be confident in the knowledge that as His disciples, we are also His ambassadors through whom He accomplishes His will on the earth. As such, He has invested in us the same authority over the works of the kingdom of darkness as He gave His original disciples when He walked the earth.

No earthly king would ever consider sending out his ambassadors to represent him without giving them authority to act in his name. Neither would our King ever consider leaving His followers and returning to heaven, without giving us the power and authority to act in His Name. He had no intention of leaving a powerless church behind to flounder in weakness and defeat. His intention is for the church to be a powerful representation and demonstration of His redeeming love and power to change the world.

That's why He sent the Holy Spirit to fill, empower, and teach His believers how to faithfully represent Him to the world, as His light in the darkness. Jesus said in John 15:5 (NKJV): *"Without Me you can do nothing."* If we have given our hearts to Christ and entered into relationship with Him, then we have the assurance of His indwelling Spirit Who strengthens us to walk with Him in victory, and enables us to become a reflection of His grace and truth.

When we are submitted to the authority of Christ, then through His Spirit within us, He empowers and teaches us how to recognize and take authority over the powers of darkness at His direction and in His strength alone when we're confronted with evil. We never seek the enemy, but because we live in a fallen world, the enemy seeks us because we belong to the One he hates. We're not immune to satan's attacks, nor can we always escape evil.

Therefore, we must arm ourselves with a knowledge of the truth as Paul instructs us in Ephesians 6 by putting on the whole armor of God. We do this through prayer, asking to be clothed and protected with His armor as a shield about us. We need to educate ourselves with the knowledge of God's Word, that we may be well-armed for the day of battle. We must be led by His Spirit and the truth of His Word, seeking His wisdom and direction in every situation. *The only way to safely prepare for spiritual warfare is through developing and maintaining an intimate relationship with Christ through spending time with Him and His Word.*

Just as our soldiers and Marines do not want to be in unequipped combat with the enemy, neither does any Christian want to be confronted by our spiritual enemies, the unseen forces of wickedness. Nevertheless, we need to be prepared for those sudden and unexpected events where we are face to face with something or someone evil. Just as our armed forces must spend months in training for combat readiness, we, too, need to be equipped and ready for the unexpected.

What I am sharing is not familiar to many Christians, nor is it a desirable subject, and the mention of it makes many frightened and unwilling to hear it. That's understandable. However, the truth is we live in an evil and fallen world and we are in a war. The fact that we don't *want* to be doesn't change the fact that we *are*. It is vitally important that we face this reality and educate ourselves, and get properly trained and equipped with the "how to" of necessary spiritual warfare. It's sad, but many Christians don't want to face the truth that we are in a war, and therefore are not equipped with the knowledge of *how* to deal with it when confronted with evil.

While the wars between nations are fought in the physical realm, there are spiritual forces behind it; and the war we are engaged in is also with unseen forces of darkness and spiritual wickedness in the heavenly places. In Ephesians 6:10-18 (NKJV) we are told:

"For we do not wrestle against flesh and blood, but against principalities, against powers, against the rulers of the darkness of this age, against spiritual hosts of wickedness in the heavenly places. Therefore, take up the whole armor of God, that you may be able to withstand in the evil day, and having done all, to stand."

These Scriptures were written for our learning with the expectation that we would take it seriously. Elsewhere in Scripture it is written:

"My people perish for lack of knowledge."

The surest way to be taken down by the enemy is to be in denial of his power, ignorant of his devices, and blind to his disguises. If you have a relationship with Christ, you have no need to fear satan because satan's authority was destroyed at the cross where Jesus shed His blood. Greater is the One Who lives in you than he (satan) who is in the world. Elsewhere in God's Word we are told that no weapon formed against you shall prosper. Though as Christians we need not fear satan, we do need to be aware of his reality and power, and alert to his devices. We need to arm ourselves with a knowledge of God's Word, which is the sword of the Spirit. God's Word and His Name are powerful weapons that have been given us to use in times of need when it is necessary to take a stand against evil. When His Word is verbally coupled with prayer in the authority of Jesus' name, it brings victory, safety, and protection.

To give you an example of how the power, authority and proper use of Jesus' Name can stop the advancement of evil when a Christian is threatened, the following are incidents which happened in my life some years ago and are living demonstrations of the victory we have in Christ. This was all a part of learning Whose I am, Who He is in me, and Who He wants to be for me in any given situation. It was also training for future ministry in prayer and spiritual warfare.

The first was when we lived in California in a duplex community. One morning as I was getting dressed, the doorbell began to ring. As it continued to ring unceasingly, I walked to the end of the hallway where I could see through the large patio door from which the drapes had been removed for cleaning. The back gate was open, and the front entryway was in view, where the back wheel of a bicycle was visible. The doorbell kept ringing, so I went to the locked front door and looked through the little hole in the door to see who it was.

There was a scraggly-looking young man on a motocross bike with some tools wrapped in the basket on his bike. He was looking first in one direction, then another, to see if anyone was watching him. He obviously and mistakenly thought no one was at home. Little did he know what was on the the other side of the door! He began using a crow bar to pry the front door open. Then he went to the front window and began prying off the screen. I was terrified for a few moments and felt my heart pounding in my chest!

Then, just as suddenly, my fear turned to rage! I thought to myself, "This is God's house! How dare he break into God's house!" Suddenly, I was trying to get the door unlocked to get at him, but fortunately, for me, I could not unlock it. At that moment, I doubled up both my fists pounding on the inside of the door as hard as I could and yelled at the top of my lungs, "In the Name of Jesus you get out of here!"

At the sound of my voice he yelled, "O.K., O.K., O.K!!" and started running.

Moments earlier I had called my friend who was the manager and told her what was going on and to send her husband. Howard was a big man, and he pulled up in his truck in time to attempt a tackle, but the kid was so scared Howard couldn't hold him down and he took off. By that time, I had successfully unlocked the door and stepped outside. (I then realized my inability to unlock the door was for my protection.)

Howard came walking across the lawn scratching his head in bewilderment, looked at me and said with a grin on his face, "What in the world did you do to him?"

"I didn't do anything to him, just yelled at him 'In the Name of Jesus, you get out of here!'"

Howard just shook his head in amazement, got back in his truck and left. That was one of the frightening lessons the Lord taught me about the authority and power Christians have in using His Name when confronted with evil. I hope that kid thought long and hard before he tried to break into someone else's house. Hopefully he was scared straight. One thing is for sure, he never forgot that day, and neither will I!

Another time when we were still living in the duplex, I would go on daily walks through a nice neighborhood not far from home, where the scenery was very beautiful and restful to the eye. Usually, I walked through the same neighborhood every day and there was one yard where two dogs were always chained in their front yard.

However, on this particular day as I walked on the opposite side of the street, I noticed they were not chained. They stared at me, never growled or barked, but slowly made their way over to me in an obvious stalking mode. I knew I was in trouble and froze in my tracks.

The huge Saint Bernard lunged at me, grabbed my wrist in his mouth and crunched down! I was so terrified I couldn't think straight, and my heart was pounding so loudly I could hear it in my ears as my knees grew weak! That is the only time in my life that I truly heard God shout at me, not audibly, but so loudly in my spirit that it rang in my ears! It was as if He had a megaphone up to my ear.

I heard the silent shout, "Use My Name, use My Name, use My Name!!"

Three times, and I finally got the message, gained my composure, never pulled my wrist away or moved, just looked the dog in the eye and said firmly and authoritatively, "In Jesus' Name, you go home!"

He dropped my wrist and the two dogs walked back to their own yard, sat down and watched me wobble down the street on shaky legs. My wrist was not broken, but badly bruised. I'll never forget that lesson.

Here is one more dog story, a short one, but the outcome shows once again the power of Jesus' Name can send evil packing. When we lived in Emmett, Idaho, next door to our house was a small trailer park. The neighbor in the trailer directly next to us had a large dog, a violation of the park rules. My husband was sick with a terminal lung disease, and the dog barked when the neighbor was working nights. I had been patient and talked with the man, but to no avail. So, one day I walked past the trailer to copy down the phone number of the manager. On the way back, the dog, who had been sleeping on the front porch, suddenly awakened and lunged off the porch after me!

Remembering my prior lesson from earlier years, with heart pounding, but without hesitation, I extended my right arm, pointing my right finger at him with authority, and yelled, "In Jesus' Name, you GO!"

He went back to his porch and sat there as I walked by with shaky knees!

I would not have asked or wished for the foregoing lessons, which were frightening and unpleasant to say the least, but during that season God was teaching me about the power and authority of using His Name and the protection He brings. For the Christian, it's a formidable weapon against the enemy when confronted by evil.

If ever you're in a dangerous situation where you are accosted or threatened, remember that all power and authority are in the Name of Jesus. He will come to your rescue if you call upon His Name. He will be there for you just as He was for me.

Chapter 15

The Battle

No better title came to mind as an apt description of the struggles we all face in life because we live in a fallen world which lies under the influence of the evil one. The fallen and corrupted condition of the world is the result of the disobedience of our original parents in the Garden of Eden, from whom all mankind since has inherited a fallen nature. One has only to look around at the chaos, corruption, brokenness, and violence to know this is true. Our own internal struggles also bear witness to this truth.

As long as we remain outside of God's kingdom, we are largely untouched by satan and are of no threat to him because we are already living in the kingdom of darkness. However, when we become a Christian, the whole scenario changes. When we become a believer and make Christ the Lord of our lives, we are transferred from the kingdom of darkness into the kingdom of light and God's Son, and that brings a declaration of war against us by the enemy of our soul, satan. When God births us into His kingdom, we are delivered onto a battleground. It bears repeating that we are in a war not of our choosing. Nevertheless, it's a reality we are forced to acknowledge and must learn to deal with. If you are a Christian, you cannot escape the conflict.

However, the great news is that Jesus' death and resurrection bought our salvation and ultimate victory over death and hell, sentencing satan to eternal punishment. Until Christ comes and enforces that sentence, putting all things under His feet, we are not left to fight the battle alone. God is with us and has provided everything we need to win through the promises of His Word, our faith, the weapons of our warfare, and the power of His indwelling Spirit.

The enemy knows his time is short in which to wreak havoc and destruction against lives, so he wages war against those whose hearts are set on loving and following God. However, he is a loser engaged in a losing battle, because every believer has The King of kings, the Lord of Hosts, fighting for and within us. And He has assured us victory in Him, which becomes ours when we believe and obey the truth of God's Word. We have a choice to make—learn to fight and win, or let the enemy trample us to defeat. The issues in the battle are God's promises and our faith. The enemy's aim is always to discredit God's Word and prevent people from coming to a saving faith in Christ. If unsuccessful in that, his next best move is to attack and attempt to destroy the believer's faith. Satan's greatest desire is to be worshiped, and when he sees he has lost another soul to God's kingdom, his assaults against the believer's mind begins.

God's aim is the salvation, healing, and transformation of our souls which can only come through faith. It is His will that we become partakers of His divine nature and become victorious in battle. 2 Peter 1:2-11 (NKJV) gives us this reassurance:

"Grace and peace be multiplied to you in the knowledge of God and of Jesus our Lord, as His divine power has given to us

all things that pertain to life and godliness, through the knowledge of Him who called us by glory and virtue, by which have been given to us exceedingly great and precious promises, that through these you may be partakers of the divine nature, having escaped the corruption that is in the world through lust...for this very reason, giving all diligence, add to your faith virtue, to virtue knowledge, to knowledge self-control, to self-control perseverance, to perseverance godliness, to godliness brotherly kindness, and to brotherly kindness love. For if these things are yours and abound, you will be neither barren nor unfruitful in the knowledge of our Lord Jesus Christ... Therefore, brethren, be even more diligent to make your call and election sure, for if you do these things you will never stumble; for so an entrance will be supplied to you abundantly into the everlasting kingdom of our Lord and Savior Jesus Christ."

He equips us for the battle, arms us with a knowledge of the truth, and fights with and for us, to bring us through to victory! Clothed in His armor, through His strength, and by His Spirit, we win!

Be assured that my intention is not to glorify satan, whom I hate with a fierce passion. Nevertheless, I find it necessary to share with you about his nature, tactics, and schemes which are aimed at destroying and aborting your life, future, the dream and purposes for which God created you. Only a knowledge of the truth can alert and equip you to deal effectively with the challenges everyone faces in life's daily arena. It is essential that you learn to discern the source behind many of the conflicts you encounter.

Most of life's challenges are a result of living in a fallen world, and the dynamics involved in all aspects of learning to live in community with others. But as the Scriptures tell us, because the whole world lies under the influence of the evil one and he is an opportunist, our enemy is intent on bringing his destructive assignments against us with purpose, passion, and design.

My hope and purpose in sharing the information in this chapter is that you would be encouraged and strengthened in your faith and find it a valuable tool to help you stand strong in the battles you face.

The most important thing to understand is our total inability to fight our battles in our own strength; we must learn to pray, seek, and depend upon God's strength and wisdom to carry us through any conflict. God is for and with us, desiring victory for us and transformation within us. Through learning to trust and obey, we become strong in the strength of the Lord.

I do not know everything about spiritual warfare, but my aim is to help you become more aware of the reality of the war we are in, to stir and challenge you to take the necessary steps of learning to equip yourself with wisdom, knowledge, faith, and skills needed in order to engage in prayers of spiritual warfare against the enemy. It is an unavoidable truth that there will be many such times.

The Lord wants to teach us how to recognize our enemy, how he operates, for the purpose of giving us the victory over him. We are promised in I John 3:8 (NKJV):

"For this purpose the Son of God was manifested, that He might destroy the works of the devil."

Most of what I've learned is from my own experiences in battles, in the trenches, through trial and error, the study, memorization, and use of Scripture; and from great teachers whom I've been privileged to sit under, men and women of great faith, who have been in tremendous spiritual battles. Having emerged victorious, they have become skilled in spiritual warfare and equipped to teach others. I've read and digested their books, and learned much from their skills and, above all, from their words of wisdom.

Wisdom tells us that none of us knows all there is to know about spiritual warfare for there is much more to learn. Oh, how we need wisdom! In pursuing the Lord each day, that is my prayer: wisdom for every moment of the day. I'm not a teacher, but a learner.

Part of my daily prayer is, "Lord, send forth Your light and Your truth; let them lead me. Fill and guide me with Your wisdom in every situation."

No one has all the truth, nor are any of us without error, for we are all in process. Wisdom also dictates that one does not engage in spiritual warfare without wise counsel. Proverbs 20:18. Eccl. 9:16-18 (NKJV) tells us that:

"Wisdom is better than strength...Wisdom is better than weapons of war."

In Proverbs 11:14 (NKJV) God's words of wisdom to us are: *"Where there is no counsel, the people fall; but in the multitude of counselors there is safety."*

"For by wise counsel you will wage your own war, and in a multitude of counselors there is safety." Proverbs 24:6 (NKJV)

I rejoice in the knowledge that everyone who believes and receives the truth about Jesus Christ and chooses to make Him the Savior and Lord of their lives has been transferred from the kingdom of darkness into the kingdom of God's dear Son,

"...having been born again, not of corruptible seed but incorruptible, through the word of God which lives and abides forever." I Peter 1:23 (NKJV)

"...knowing that you were not redeemed with corruptible things, like silver or gold, but with the precious blood of Christ, as of a lamb without blemish and without spot." I Peter 1:18,19 (NKJV)

Every chapter of this book has been a joy to write until the ones dealing with spiritual warfare. As I began each of these devoted to spiritual battles and satan's tactics, I had a tremendous struggle concentrating, experiencing unusual heaviness, fatigue and depression. I soon realized there was resistance and interference in the spiritual realm from the enemy who definitely opposes the truth and any means God wants to use to bring people to a saving knowledge of the truth through His Son Jesus Christ.

I had been doing a lot of writing the days before undertaking the afore-mentioned chapters, and thought it would be good to take a break from the book. However, nothing I tried satisfied—not television, music, reading the Scriptures, praying, *not anything*. The awful weight of heaviness would not lift from me. My thought was I wouldn't be able to concentrate, but I picked up my laptop, said a prayer, and began to write.

It was early afternoon and I kept writing, going from the Get Well chapter right into More Than Conquerors, not stopping until I finished at 11:00 p.m. The longer I wrote, the more the heaviness lifted from me until at the conclusion that night, it was entirely gone and I felt a release, sense of well-being, and peace of mind, knowing it was right. Though there was harassment from the enemy, it was also evident that God's hand was so heavy upon me that nothing I tried could satisfy until I was doing what He had been wanting all along. He always knows what's best, and His thoughts are certainly higher than ours. So much for what I thought was a "good" idea. Sometimes good ideas are not always God's ideas and this was a case which reminded me of how important it is to keep my thoughts submitted to the Holy Spirit, praying and listening to Him, and not giving in to distractions. He will always instruct us in the way to go if we ask, listen, and wait. It reminds me of His promise in Psalm 32:8 (NKJV):

"I will instruct you and teach you in the way you should go. I will guide you with My eye."

Settling myself down to write those chapters was an unusual struggle and, after consulting others, I had confirmations that the enemy was putting up a fight, trying to cause distraction to hinder the completion of this book. But God is so faithful to keep on prompting and pressing us toward His assignments for us. The tasks He assigns are not without struggle or opposition because our flesh is weak and our unseen enemy is very real. Our enemy, satan, hates Christ and everything He stands for.

Some of the greatest achievements in life have been birthed through great opposition, struggle, and sacrifice. The battle in this world and in our lives is not a physical one but is fought in the unseen spiritual realm between the kingdom of light and the kingdom of darkness, the kingdom of God and the kingdom of satan, good opposed by evil. Every kingdom has a king. Jesus Christ is God, Creator and Savior of mankind, the King of kings and Lord of lords. In Him is all authority, dominion and power. As Creator, He has the right to rule, and the day will come in which He will destroy satan, the king over all evil and those who serve him.

The Scriptures are clear regarding the choice each of us will make in life about whom we will serve:

"No one can serve two masters; for either he will hate the one and love the other, or else he will be loyal to the one and despise the other. You cannot serve God and mammon."
Matthew 6:24 (NKJV)

The word "mammon" is translated as riches, material wealth. God is the provider of every good thing, and is in no way opposed to material wealth. He blessed and poured out much wealth upon His servants as recorded in the Old Testament. Abraham, Isaac, Jacob, and others were very wealthy by the world's standards, but the key to their success was the fact that their master was God with Whom they were rightly related and served obediently. He was their greatest priority. They were not seeking material wealth, but God Himself. Material wealth is not a problem, but the *desire to be rich* becomes a snare to the human heart. The Bible also says in Psalm 84:11 (NKJV) that

"No good thing will He withhold from those who walk uprightly."

God's promise is *if you will "seek first the kingdom of God and His righteousness, all these things shall be added to you."*
Matt. 6:33 (NKJV).

In Exodus 20, we find the first of the Ten Commandments in which God states: *"You shall have no other gods before me."*

Anyone or anything we love and desire more than God Himself constitutes idolatry. Therefore, the real aim in this battle between good and evil is our souls, who will be our master, whom we will serve, and where we will spend eternity. God has left the choice with us, one in which He does not to impose His will, though it is the greatest desire of His heart that we would choose to love and serve Him.

Jesus said in Matt.12:30 (NKJV): *"He who is not with Me is against Me."* If you think you don't have to choose which kingdom you will serve in or who will be your master, you already have. We all serve someone.

Our minds are a battleground in which our battles are won or lost according to our thoughts and what we choose to believe, whether it be the truth, or deception from satan, whom the Scripture refers to as the "father of lies." He is the master deceiver whose chief aim is to turn people away from the truth, away from Jesus Who is the way, the truth and life. Just as the devil deceived Eve in the Garden of Eden, (Gen. 3), resulting in disobedience, the fall, and the severance of their relationship with God, so he is still planting lies in people's minds today and is able to persuade them it is truth. Why is he able to achieve this? Because *the lie agrees with the desire of their flesh. His lies satisfy the desire of their will.*

The terrible thing about deception is that those who are deceived believe what they think is truth. Therefore, if a person believes a lie, he or she will walk in it and live it, thinking they are believing and walking in the truth, when in fact they are walking farther away from God and the truth that can set them free. Once they are deceived, they are fair game for further lies to invade and influence their thoughts, until a mindset is established which becomes a mental stronghold of thoughts that rule their mind.

What is a stronghold? The dictionary defines the word as: "a place having strong defenses; fortified places; a place where a group having certain views, attitudes, etc. is concentrated." We should strive to make God our only stronghold. When our minds and hearts are submitted to God and His Word, we are growing in the grace and knowledge of Him; our minds are being renewed to think in alignment with His thoughts and His truth teaches us to think with a new mind set. God becomes our stronghold, where we become occupied with thoughts of Him and things of eternal value. He becomes our place of refuge and strong defense. His truth becomes our standard by which we live and make choices that lead to life and blessing.

Good News

The good news is that Jesus came to set the captives free! In Isaiah 61:1 (NKJV) Jesus says of Himself:

"The Spirit of the Lord God is upon Me, because the Lord has anointed Me to preach good tidings to the poor; He has sent Me to heal the brokenhearted, to proclaim liberty to the captives and the opening of the prison to those who are bound."

In 2 Timothy 2:24-26 (NKJV) we are instructed:

"And a servant of the Lord must not quarrel but be gentle to all, able to teach, patient, in humility correcting those who are in opposition, if God perhaps will grant them repentance, so that they may know the truth and that they may come to their senses and escape the snare of the devil, having been taken captive by him to do his will."

Jesus was sent to save, heal, and deliver us from the enemy's schemes and snares, which are presented to us through his lies. The only two things satan can do is lie to you and accuse you. He is referred to in Scripture as the "accuser of the brethren," recorded in Revelation 12:10 (NKJV): *"for the accuser of our brethren, who accused them before our God day and night, has been cast down."*

The devil's aim is not only to lie to you in the hope of destroying your faith in God, but double-sided in that he couples his lies about God with accusations about yourself, reminding and accusing you of past sins and failures. He doesn't want you to know and believe that the blood of Jesus forgives all your sins, cleanses you from all unrighteousness and removes all the guilt and shame of the past, nor does he want you to know the truth of God's promise in Rev.12:11 (NKJV) and our victory over him:

"And they overcame him by the blood of the Lamb and by the word of their testimony."

In I Peter 5:8,9 (NIV) we are urged to:

"Be self-controlled and alert. Your enemy the devil prowls around like a roaring lion looking for someone to devour. Resist him, standing firm in the faith, because you know that your brothers throughout the world are undergoing the same kind of sufferings."

It is imperative to guard your heart and mind against all deception, learning to listen to and walk in the truth so you will be in a position to receive God's best and all that He plans for your future. Even though your soul may be saved and you will spend eternity with Him, it is possible to miss the fullness of all He wants to do and accomplish in your life for His glory. We need to pursue and press into Him. Have faith in God! His plans for your future are always beyond your own abilities and greater than your hopes. His desire is to see you become in character like His Son in order to fulfill all He created you to be for the advancement of His kingdom and glory on this earth. Paul said in Philippians 3:13,14 (NIV), speaking of himself, but also for all of us:

"Brothers, I do not consider myself yet to have taken hold of it, but one thing I do: forgetting what is behind and straining toward what is ahead, I press on toward the goal to win the prize for which God has called me heavenward in Christ Jesus."

Your belief system, what you think about yourself and God, is extremely important because it affects all your decisions, determines the path you will take and your destiny. In order to fulfill God's plan for your present and future, it is important that you see yourself as He sees you. It's important that you know His thoughts toward you.

Proverbs 23:7 (NKJV) tells us: *"For as he thinks in his heart, so is he."* This is why it is vitally important that you feed your mind on the *truth* of God's Word.

We are instructed in Romans 12:2 (NKJV):

"And do not be conformed to this world, but be transformed by the renewing of your mind, that you may prove what is that good and acceptable and perfect will of God."

Also, Ephesians 4:23 (NKJV) instructs us to *"be renewed in the spirit of your mind."* Renewing your mind requires faith in God and believing the Bible is true, faith that He loves you and wants to bless you, that He has a plan and a future for your life. Hebrews 11:6 (NIV) states:

"And without faith it is impossible to please God, because anyone who comes to him must believe that he exists and that he rewards those who earnestly seek him."

Authority and Power: The Difference

Although I have written the truth about satan's reality and his goal to deceive and destroy lives, my much larger purpose is to declare the greatness of God's love for us and His triumph over the evil one when He sent Christ to the cross on our behalf. At the cross, satan's authority to use his power was destroyed by the blood of Jesus poured out there; it sealed his doom and sentenced him to defeat and eternal punishment.

It is important to understand the difference between the words *authority* and *power*. What was destroyed at the cross through the blood of Christ was not satan's power but his authority to use that power. Power is defined as: Great ability to do, act, or affect strongly; vigor; force; strength. Authority is: The right to give commands, enforce obedience, take action; jurisdiction, the right to rule, delegated authority. Since satan's right to use his power was stripped and removed from him, he no longer has any authority to use his power, but he will, *unless and until he is stopped.* He is a usurper, a trespasser, and thief who comes to steal, kill, and destroy.

If you are a Christian, that is, if you have a personal relationship with Jesus Christ as your Savior and He is the Lord of your life, *you have the indwelling power of the Holy Spirit and have been given authority over satan and all his evil works.* This is so important to understand because it is a key factor in learning your true identity in Christ. The truth is that He has vested in you, His disciple, the same authority over the works of evil as He vested in His early disciples. In Mark 3:14,15 (NKJV) we read:

"Then He appointed twelve, that they might be with Him and that He might send them out to preach, and to have power to heal sicknesses and to cast out demons."

The word *power* here in this usage is defined in Strong's Concordance. In the Greek, it is translated exogenous which means authority or right to act, delegated authority.

Quoting from the *Word Wealth* explanation of the word *power* in verse 15: "Jesus had the *exousia* to forgive sin, heal sicknesses and cast out demons. *Exousia* is the right to use *dynamos* "might." Jesus gave His followers *exousia* to preach, teach, heal, and deliver (v. 15), and that authority has never been rescinded. (John 14:12) Powerless ministries become powerful against the kingdom of darkness when they discover the *exousia* (authority) power resident in the Name of Jesus and the blood of Jesus." Yes, Jesus selected, appointed, and commissioned the apostles with the power of the Holy Spirit for the special task of establishing and governing the church, but the same *exousia* power of the Holy Spirit continued and still continues to be poured out today upon His Church, upon every born-again believer who is wholly devoted to Him. I believe He vests His authority in those who are yielded and fully submitted to His authority and filled with His Holy Spirit, those with whom He can entrust the stewardship of His gifts, grace and ministry of the Holy Spirit.

I've shared these thoughts with the prayer that the Lord will use them to bring understanding of the important truth that satan's authority *was destroyed* at the cross by the powerful blood of Jesus. When we receive and embrace Christ as our Savior and the Lord of our lives, we are no longer under the enemy's rule. He has no authority over us. We've been redeemed by the blood of the Lamb. The enemy truly is a defeated foe and *the Lord wants us to live as though we know and believe it! Never should we run scared of satan's attacks!*

Though I've felt it necessary to write about his nature and schemes in this chapter, *never should we give him glory by declaring all the things he is doing; rather when we see him working, be aware of it, yet focus on and declare the greatness of our God, declaring the truth of God's Word and prayer! Remember Whose you are, and Who lives in you! Greater is Christ Who is in you than he (the enemy) who is in the world!*

God's Word is such good news! It is the greatest weapon we've been given against the lies of the enemy. His promises of absolute truth cover every need we have. His Word is eternal, alive, active, and as powerful today as it was when Jesus spoke it to satan during His temptation in the wilderness. God has a Scripture promise for every situation we encounter and it is the only thing that can counter and defeat satan's lies.

Jesus gave us the supreme example of how we can defeat the enemy. Luke 4 gives the account of His temptation and how He responded. It is important to know that when Jesus resisted satan's temptations, He did not use His deity or position as God to defeat him. Rather, he met the tempter as a man full of the Holy Spirit and the knowledge of the Scriptures, wholly submitted to His Father. He was showing us the way to have victory over temptations in the wilderness times of our lives.

In Luke 4, you will note that Jesus' response to each challenge from satan was verbally declaring the Scripture and preceding it with *"It is written..."* Jesus knew Who He was, where He was going, and that satan was no match for God. When He spoke, it was with full knowledge and confidence in the authority and victory He had over the evil one. The day will come when every knee will bow and every tongue will confess Jesus Christ is Lord.

To know the truth, you must read, feed, and renew your mind, using the Scriptures, and asking the Holy Spirit to give you understanding and bring your thoughts into harmony with His. When your mind is filled with negative and faith-destroying thoughts, *become aware of the real source from which they come.*

Next, *find verses of Scripture that speak the truth to the lie.* Then *commit them to memory, ready to speak the truth when you need to make a declaration of faith. In prayer, ask the Lord to help you remember His words and make them reality in your heart.* In Ephesians 6:10-18 the armor of God is pictured as that of a Roman soldier and the Word described as the "sword of the Spirit."

We read in II Corinthians 10:4,5 (NKJV):

"For the weapons of our warfare are not carnal (of the flesh) but mighty in God for pulling down strongholds, casting down arguments and every high thing that exalts itself against the knowledge of God, bringing every thought into captivity to the obedience of Christ."

Although the Word is pictured as the sword of the soldier's armor and referred to as the "sword of the Spirit," in any conflict we will only be successful when we draw it out of its sheath and wield it (speak it) in faith at the enemy, just as Jesus verbally hurled the Word at the enemy. That is why we should memorize the Word and be ready to use it when needed. To have victory over the thought life, we must put faith into action and follow Jesus' example. We cannot afford to be passive or indifferent to satan's attacks when he approaches us with his lies and accusations.

And approach us he will. He is an opportunist who capitalizes on our ignorance and takes advantage of any passivity or indifference which he considers an open invitation and an avenue to pursue for the advancement of his kingdom. When we are in a time of extreme stress, exhaustion, or crisis, we are most vulnerable to his assaults and especially need to guard our hearts. When Jesus was in the Garden of Gethsemane before His death, He found His disciples sleeping, and said to Peter:

"What? Could you not watch with Me one hour? Watch and pray, lest you enter into temptation. The spirit indeed is willing, but the flesh is weak." Matt. 26:41 (NKJV)

Since all of our battles are won or lost in our minds, I repeat, what we think is crucial to our victory or defeat. Guard your mind and heart!

In God's Word, the pieces of armor are listed in Ephesians 6:14-18 (NIV); I wish to emphasize the first one and how crucial it is: *"Stand firm then, with the belt of truth buckled around your waist."*

The first piece of armor is the belt of truth. It is significant because the belt of the Roman soldier's armor held all the rest of the armor in place. How vitally important it is that we believe and know the *truth,* without which none of the other armor will save us. Every day my prayer is that God would be the guardian and keeper of my thoughts, and clothe me with His full armor. However, this morning in my exhaustion I forgot to.

My walk this morning was a classic example of the mental and verbal warfare described in II Corinthians 10:4,5 above. I experienced the battle with negative thoughts about myself, thinking of losing strength, growing too old, it's too late for God to fulfill His dream for me, etc. I awakened with unusual fatigue due to a restless night of broken sleep, making my commitment to walk even more difficult.

As I put on my walking shoes, I thanked God for the day and prayed for strength to walk as He wanted me to. As I started out, the negative thoughts began, thoughts that were faith-destroying and untrue. So, I began to speak into the atmosphere the truth of God's Word against the lies as I walked, the kind of self-talk that produces faith, life, and renewed energy. I needed to hear these words of truth coming from my mouth, such as,

"Thanks be to God who always gives me the victory through the Lord Jesus Christ;" "I can do all things through Christ who strengthens me;" "I am strong in the Lord and in the power of His might because greater is He who is in me than he who is in the world;" and *"no weapon formed against me shall prosper."*

For the entire walk I spoke the truth of the Word, and then commanded every thought to come into obedience to the Lord Jesus Christ and the Word of God. By the time I walked the mile, my mind was clear and alert, my spirit uplifted, and my body felt better. These Scriptures are all part of what I refer to as my arsenal, verses committed to memory over the years, and they are ready for recall at a moment's notice.

Incidents such as what I experienced this morning are why we need to have the Word written in our heart and memory. When I shared the above incident at a prayer meeting recently and mentioned that it was going in the book as an example of the power of God's Word and the way He rescues us in situations, someone there said, and I quote him, "And He is still rescuing you."

So true! He is indeed, and I praise Him for His faithfulness.

The Weapons of our Warfare

God's intention for us is not that we should simply survive the assaults of the enemy, but much more. His desire is that we live in bold confidence and victory over the works of darkness and evil, and become a reflection of the reality, beauty, and power of the Lord Jesus Christ living in us. God has given us many weapons of warfare with which to do battle against the enemy.

The first part of our defense and weaponry is listed in Ephesians 6:10-18 (NKJV) as the armor of God and describes the battle we face:

"Finally, my brethren, be strong in the Lord and in the power of His might. Put on the whole armor of God, that you may be able to stand against the wiles of the devil. For we do not wrestle against flesh and blood, but against principalities, against powers, against the rulers of the darkness of this age, against spiritual hosts of wickedness in the heavenly places. Therefore take up the whole armor of God, that you may be able to withstand in the evil day, and having done all, to stand. Stand therefore, having girded your waist with truth, having put on the breastplate of righteousness, and having shod your feet with the preparation of the gospel of peace, above all, taking the shield of faith with which you will be able to quench all the fiery darts of the wicked one. And take the helmet of salvation and the sword of the Spirit which is the Word of God; praying always with all prayer and supplication in the Spirit, being watchful to this end with all perseverance and supplication for all the saints."

Though these are part of the armor of God, they are not the only equipment God has made available to us. Asking God to keep us clothed with His armor and filled with His Spirit should be part of our daily prayer. This is simply putting on the nature of Christ by asking the Father to make us like Him. For every piece of the armor listed, there is a Scripture verse which states who Christ is: *He is the truth, He is our righteousness, our peace, our shield of faith, our salvation, our sword of the Spirit, the Living Word. He is our Intercessor Who sits at the right hand of the Father always interceding for us,* and has given us the responsibility and weapon of prayer as we intercede for others.

Other weapons which carry power against the enemy are the blood of Jesus, verbal praise with thanksgiving, and declaring God's promises which apply to our situation, singing praises, worshiping God, and fasting with prayer. And after we've done all we know to do, we stand in faith, believing. We are told in I John 5:4,5 (NKJV):

"And this is the victory that has overcome the world—our

*faith. Who is he who overcomes the world, but he who believes
that Jesus is the Son of God?"*

The following story from II Chronicles 20 is one of my
favorite examples of how God brings victory to those who trust
and obey Him. Sometimes God will say to us that we need not
fight the battle because it is His, as He did when King
Jehoshaphat and the people of Judah were surrounded with
multitudes of armies from Syria who were plotting to crush
them.

The first thing the king did was to seek the Lord, call the
people together, and proclaim a fast. Then, verbally, before all
the people, He poured his heart out to God, reminding Him of
His faithfulness and greatness toward them in times past. They
were all gathered before the Lord when the Spirit of the Lord
came upon Jahaziel who received a word from the Lord for
them in their distress. They were told not to be afraid because
the battle was not theirs, but God's.

Then Jehoshaphat bowed his head with his face to the ground
and all the inhabitants of Jerusalem bowed before the Lord,
worshiping Him. God gave them the strategy to put the singers
and worshipers before their army and go before them. As they
went out before the army singing, *"Praise the Lord, for His
mercy endures forever,"* the Lord set ambushes against the
people of Syria who had come against them, and they were
defeated.

This is an example of how God used the power of singing
praise and worship to Him to destroy the enemy. It is also a
powerful principle that works in our behalf today. I've
experienced the victory of it on more than one occasion. Even
though this is an Old Testament incident, God's principles are
unchanging, His power and faithfulness undiminished, and it is
recorded for our learning.

Several years ago, I was sitting with my Bible in my lap,
looking at Psalm 100. As I read, I was feeling very oppressed,
almost in depression. I read the verses out loud, and when I

came to the second verse the verse said to come before His presence with singing. So I did, and as soon as I opened my mouth to sing to Him, the awful feeling of oppression lifted from me and I felt at peace and joyful again. The enemy's oppression was driven away by my obedience to God's Word for that very moment—to sing praise to Him which brought me into His presence. I have found that obedience to the Word brings our freedom.

Though this next item is not considered a weapon, I include it here because it is another powerful place of provision and protection for the Christian—partaking of the Lord's Supper, often. Nothing is more powerful than the blood of Jesus and the power of His cross. This has become a part of my daily worship and communion with the Lord, and a powerful strengthener for my spirit, soul, and body each day.

Far from being a ritual, it is a holy and precious time of communion and fellowship with Jesus at the table to which He invites me. It is the table of my King, which He prepares for me in the presence of my enemies, as stated in Psalm 23. He offers this invitation to all of His children, a tangible ordinance whereby we come into His presence to commune with Him in thanksgiving for His death on the cross where He sacrificed His body for our healing, and His blood for our sins. We should also come to celebrate His glorious resurrection which gives the power of His risen life to live in our mortal bodies here and now.

Romans 8:11 (NIV) gives us this promise:

"And if the Spirit of him who raised Jesus from the dead is living in you, he who raised Christ from the dead will also give life to your mortal bodies through his Spirit, who lives in you."

I find the older I get, the more I need this precious time at His table where I truly do receive fresh spiritual and physical strength and vitality for each day.

In order to walk in victory and confidence with Him, we must first learn the same principles Jesus taught His disciples when

He trained them. He was training them to do the same works He did, preparing and equipping them for all things, even encounters with enemy spirits. They went with Him everywhere, observing Him as He healed many of physical afflictions and delivered others from demonic oppression. *But before He sent them out to do the same works He did, He gave them instructions to be wise as serpents and harmless as doves.* Matt.10:16 (NKJV) says:

"Behold, I send you out as sheep in the midst of wolves. Therefore be wise as serpents and harmless as doves."

Our spiritual victory in all situations we encounter is dependent upon several qualities that must have pre-eminence in us.

First, we must have discernment to clearly hear the voice of the Holy Spirit and go only into the conflict where He sends us, with the grace and attitude of Christ's humility and wisdom. It is of vital importance to understand there are some battles in the spiritual realm that God wants us to keep our hands off, and territory that is off-limits to us and where He has not instructed us to go, territory over which we have not been given authority or jurisdiction. These are situations where our responsibility is to pray in faith believing, situations where the prayer of faith becomes our warfare, praying for God's kingdom to come, His will to be done in the situation on the earth as it is in heaven.

Second, part of the training as a prayer warrior is learning how, in prayer, to bind the forces of evil from people and situations, and ask the Holy Spirit to bring truth and lead them.

Third, faith is an important part of our armor and an integral weapon of our warfare which must be given its rightful place of key importance. However, there is danger that faith without wisdom becomes nothing less than presumption, leading to sure defeat and getting badly beaten up by the spiritual forces of darkness.

It is possible in some situations to have exercised faith wrongly when we should have sought God for the wisdom of

His way in it. I cannot over-emphasize the need for wisdom and humility to guide us. May God keep us from pride and presumptuous sins. Though it may be well-intentioned, nothing could be worse than to blindly enter into an encounter with the forces of evil in an attitude of presumption. Some well-meaning Christians have presumptuously and zealously entered into warfare with the enemy and as a result have taken a serious beating.

Our absolute priority, in order to have success in spiritual warfare, must be to have an intimate relationship with Christ through the knowledge of His Word and His Spirit, walking in His truth, humility, and wisdom. We also need to be trained by those who live by His Spirit, and walk in integrity, humility, and wisdom in the knowledge of God's Word and ways. Many have fallen as a result of ignorance and zeal without wisdom or training. We must learn to recognize and discern the assaults of the enemy and how to apply God's wisdom and grace in our responses to those who unknowingly are being influenced by him.

In Ephesians 5:15-18 (NKJV) we are cautioned:

"See then that you walk circumspectly, not as fools but as wise, redeeming the time, because the days are evil. Therefore do not be unwise, but understand what the will of the Lord is, and do not be drunk with wine in which is dissipation, but be filled with the Spirit."

The word *circumspectly* means to walk cautiously, sensitively, as a person would walk through thorny terrain. To be filled with the Spirit in this verse means to continually be filled. I urge you to meditate on the words from Proverbs 4:7 (NKJV):

"Wisdom is the principal thing; therefore get wisdom and in all your getting, get understanding."

If you have never read the story of David and Goliath in the book of I Samuel 17 of the Bible, I encourage you to read it now. It is the account of how David, a young shepherd assigned to his father's flocks, who later became Israel's future king, fought and killed the Philistine giant, Goliath, who was over nine feet tall. The Philistines had gathered their forces for war against the Israelites, and Goliath was their champion. He stepped out, taunting and shouting threats at Israel. Then David came on the scene, sent by his father to check on his older brothers who were with Israel's army. When David heard the taunts and threats of Goliath, he was angered at the insults against Israel and God Himself, and sought permission from King Saul to fight him. Because David knew that God was with him and earlier had helped him kill a lion and a bear, he had absolute confidence that God would give the giant into his hands. David ran to meet Goliath, and placing a stone in his sling, with deadly aim, he hurled it at Goliath's head, brought the giant down, and beheaded him. Because of previous smaller victories, David had faith and confidence in God's faithfulness and power to deliver Israel from her enemies. As he ran to meet Goliath, in his heart David *knew by faith* he was looking at a dead man. His eyes weren't on the size of the giant, but on the greatness and faithfulness of his God. David trusted in God for the victory, and God gave it.

The point here is that there will be giants in all our lives, obstacles of overwhelming proportions, perhaps personal character flaws, loss of a loved one, impossible circumstances for which there is no hope apart from God's divine intervention, challenges in whatever form they might appear. They will be so huge that only trusting in God's power and faithfulness can bring victory. Apart from God's miracle-working grace in our own hearts, in others, and His hand at work in the situation, there can be no victory, for without Him we can do nothing.

However, God allows giants in our lives not to destroy us but to make us strong where we are weak, to show His greatness on our behalf, and His faithfulness to help us overcome in victory. He brings situations to us in which we are forced to fight, forced to exercise faith like a muscle—the more it is exercised the stronger you become. Every challenge we encounter is an opportunity to grow in our faith as we turn each struggle over to Him, learning that the key to our victory lies in our willingness to surrender the idea of trying to conquer it in our own strength, which produces nothing but fruitless exhaustion. God's plan is for us to win over evil and the challenges in life, and in the process become transformed in our character to be like Jesus. He is bigger and greater than any giant you face. Don't fear your Goliaths, but face them in the strength of the Lord with confident faith that you're not fighting the battle alone. He is with you and in you to fight for you, all for the purpose of bringing victory, blessing for you, and glory for His Name. This is why in I Timothy 6:12 (NKJV) we are urged to: *"Fight the good fight of faith."* With Him, we win!

****

There comes a time in all our lives when we become battle-weary, feel defeated and discouraged. Sometimes we suffer loss, and in those times we feel anything but victorious. Our lives are journeys, a combination of mountaintops and valleys, victory and defeat, laughter and tears, sorrow and joy, faith and doubt, weakness and strength, seasons and events.

Right now as I'm writing, my heart is filled with peace and joy in the knowledge of God's love for me and the confidence that He is bringing this book to conclusion. However, as I mentioned earlier, less than a week ago I was experiencing deep depression. My mind was being assaulted with lies. It was a battle, and required a tremendous effort to do the mental and verbal warfare necessary to break and lift that darkness from me. I sent out calls to friends who are prayer warriors, and many prayers were sent up and still are being sent up for me as I write.

Today, I am experiencing victory. But the last two weeks have been such a struggle! A dear friend of mine who is a counselor, therapist, and prayer warrior, encouraged me with assurance that the onslaught against me was all about the book finishing, that the enemy was putting up a fight because of its contents which expose him for what he is. I saved her voice message and have listened to it several times as a means of staying encouraged by her words of truth. Thank God for His faithful people who have kept me lifted up in prayer!

It is the power of prayer that has played a major part in this book becoming a reality. The truth is, because we are in these human frames, no matter how much we love the Lord and how closely we walk with Him, there will be times when we will feel the brunt of the enemy's assaults. But satan is the loser. Christ is my victory!

Praise God that according to God's Word, no weapon formed against me shall prosper, and if God is for us who can be against us! One thing has been made quite clear. God has allowed these harassments from the enemy to make sure I would be writing from experience and learn to press through to complete this assignment He called me to. He never leaves anything out!

I can honestly say I don't remember a time when I've experienced such bouts of oppression, even while spending ample time with Him in His Word, in prayer, and praise, with an awareness of His presence with me, doing everything I knew to do to stay above the onslaught. This is why prayer for one another becomes so crucial and absolutely necessary to the accomplishment of God's will in each of our lives. It's why God made His people into a family who cares for one another. We were made for one another, and need relationships with family and community. None of us can fulfill our destiny alone.

If you are battle-weary and experiencing burn-out, or are exhausted from the struggles of life, the very best thing you can do is accept Jesus' invitation from Matt. 11:28-30 (NKJV) where He says, *"Come to Me, all you who labor and are heavy laden, and I will give you rest."* We will find the beginning of our rest when we purposely take that step of turning our thoughts to Him. It is always the desire of His heart to give you rest and refreshing, but it takes time and practice to quiet ourselves in His presence and give ourselves the grace to simply rest in Him.

To practice His presence is the opposite of our twenty-first century pace of living which promotes constant activity. However, He is just a heartbeat and a prayer away, and His presence is always with us. To enter His rest requires our heart's attention.

Is. 40:31 (NKJV) is a comfort and a promise to those who will take time to rest and wait in God's presence:

"But those who wait on the Lord shall renew their strength; they shall mount up with wings like eagles. They shall run and not be weary. They shall walk and not faint."

On my walk this morning, my thoughts turned to those who have grown weary and may feel as though life has left them defeated. None of us walk in one hundred percent victory all the time, or ever will, this side of heaven. As mentioned earlier, we are all in process, but God has our victory in His mind and heart. Even when we fail in our struggles and weaknesses, His love is with us and His grace sufficient, just as He told Paul in 2 Cor.12:9 (NKJV) when he asked God to remove his thorn in the flesh: *"And He said to me, 'My grace is sufficient for you for My strength is made perfect in weakness.' "*

It doesn't matter how many times we stumble or fall; *it is the direction our hearts have determined to go that matters to Him.* In this race called life some of us will cross the finish line with scars on our knees. It's not how you start life or the background from which you come that matters. *What really matters is how you finish.*

As I continued in my walk, I visualized people with weary hearts, walking with no spring in their step or sense of purpose, perhaps because of where I've been at different seasons of my life. My thoughts went to Psalm 24 and how the Lord used this portion of it to impact my heart with His refreshing presence and powerful touch. In weariness I lifted my heart and soul to Him, asking Him to come in—and He did, breathing fresh life into my spirit, turning weariness to refreshing, encouragement, and hope.

He is so faithful to hear our cries and to come to our help. The wonderful truth of this psalm applies to our hearts and minds, and essentially declares that whoever opens up to Him, wherever He is welcomed, the King of glory enters in. As I share these Scriptures, if your heart can relate to this need, I encourage you to make these verses a personal prayer of your own. He longs to come into the voids in your life and fill them with the glory and peace of His presence as you invite Him. Jesus is the King of glory.

Ps. 24:7-10 (NKJV):

"Lift up your heads, O you gates! And be lifted up, you everlasting doors! And the King of glory shall come in. Who is this King of glory? The Lord strong and mighty. The Lord mighty in battle! Lift up your heads, O you gates! Lift up you everlasting doors! And the King of glory shall come in. Who is this King of glory? The Lord of hosts. He is the King of glory!"

This is our God! This is our King, our God Who fights for us!

"We give You thanks O Lord God Almighty, The One who is and who was and who is to come, Because You have taken Your great power and reigned." Rev.11:17 (NKJV)

"Then the seventh angel sounded: And there were loud voices in heaven, saying, 'The kingdoms of this world have become the kingdoms of our Lord and of His Christ, and He shall reign forever and ever!'" Revelation 11:15 (NKJV)

****

Chapter 16

'More Than Conquerors

It is with great joy and satisfaction this final chapter is being written. My prayer is that God's heart is satisfied with what has been shared. I trust that hearts will be awakened and moved toward Him with the realization of His great love for them and the desire to know Him. When I knew the Lord was commissioning me to write His story, there were many experiences to draw from, and I have prayed much for His guidance to cover every part of it as I've committed my mind and hands to His leading.

At the beginning of the book I described the dream God gave me when I was just ten years old. Many times I've wondered why He would choose me to be the recipient of such a powerful and life-changing dream—Jesus walking across storm-tossed waves and shark-infested waters to grip my hand and walk me back across the water to the other shore. He knew my heart, and saw my fears, and came just when I needed Him most. It was shortly after that I committed my life to Him. I mention it again now because of the message it contains for everyone who may read it. I believe whatever He does in our lives is used to bring encouragement to others, not just for our benefit. In a way I've saved the best for last, at least for me.

The meaning of the dream unfolded as I lived life, with the stormy crises, overwhelming circumstances, and losses that came. Jesus has been with me in the center of every one, and even now has me gripped by His hand. I think of all He has brought me through and how, in my confusion as a youngster, He knew the dream was needed to bring me to Him. I'm sure He saw my weaknesses and frailty, and in His compassion took action to save me. He means more than life to me. He *is* my life, and in Him I live and move and have my being.

Phil. 1:21 (NIV) is the verse that I live by:

"For to me to live is Christ, and to die is gain."

Several years ago, I was given the privilege of speaking to a women's group in a neighboring town. As I was asking the Lord what He wanted me to say that would be the message of His heart, the remembrance of the dream came to my mind again when I was walking along the canal. I had always thought the dream was just for me, but God gave me a larger picture and the realization that it was a message for others as well, which would bring hope and encouragement to them as it has to me.

He gave me the understanding that as our Creator the intention of His heart for each of us is that we be victorious in life with all of its challenges and disappointments. It is His plan and promise that if we will make Jesus the Savior and Lord of our lives, He will take our hand and walk us through all the storms and circumstances of life, strengthening us to overcome everything that the world and the enemy can throw at us. If you will make room for Him and let Him be the Lord of your life, He will never fail you.

His Word is filled with promises that tell you not to fear, because He is with you. Isaiah 41:10 (NIV) is one of my favorites in which He promises:

"So do not fear, for I am with you; do not be dismayed, for I am your God. I will strengthen you and help you; I will uphold you with my righteous right hand."

He is our shield and our defense. As our Creator, He has all power and authority over life. We were created to overcome! When He has us in the grip of His hand, with our hearts committed to Him, nothing can separate us from His love and we become more than conquerors in life. He will take us safely through, and with Him we win! Not only is He with us, but He is *in* us, Christ the hope of glory, through the power of His Spirit.

Paul said in Phil. 4:13 (NIV): *"I can do all things through Christ who strengthens me."*

In all of our struggles, He is always with us, ready to lift us up with His strength, guide us as our Shepherd, and comfort us with His Presence. We have only to believe and turn our eyes upon Him, draw near to Him and He will draw near to us. The Lord knows how to rescue you from your trials or strengthen you in them. I encourage you to give all your cares and worries to Him, because He cares about what happens to you. If Christ dwells in you, the Scripture in I John 4:4 (NKJV) declares:

"He who is in you is greater than he who is in the world."

Some of my favorite Scriptures which have given me great comfort during difficult times are Romans 8:31-37 (NIV):

"What, then, shall we say in response to this? If God is for us, who can be against us? He who did not spare his own Son, but gave him up for us all, how will He not also, along with Him, graciously give us all things? Who will bring any charge against those whom God has chosen? It is God who justifies. Who is he that condemns? Christ Jesus, who died—more than that, who was raised to life—is at the right hand of God and is also interceding for us. Who shall separate us from the love of Christ? Shall trouble or hardship or persecution or famine or nakedness or danger or sword? As it is written: 'For your sake we face death all day long; we are considered as sheep to be

slaughtered.' No, in all these things we are more than
conquerors through him who loved us. For I am convinced that
neither death nor life, neither angels nor demons, neither the
present nor the future, nor any powers, neither height nor
depth, nor anything else in all creation, will be able to separate
us from the love of God that is in Christ Jesus our Lord."

Christ's Return

My heart is filled with anticipation of Christ's return as I think
about the condition of our world and the utter chaos that seems
to be everywhere: natural disasters, famines, wars, persecution
of Christians, anti-Semitism, spiritual and moral decay in our
own culture, and throughout the world. All these things are
signs of the times which point to the soon return of the Lord
Jesus Christ and these are set forth in the Scriptures. I believe,
as do a large number of people, that we are living in what the
Scriptures describe as the last days.

No one knows the day or the hour of Christ's return, but one
thing we do know is what the words of Paul tell us in Romans
13:11 (NKJV):

"...that now it is high time to awake out of sleep; for now
our salvation is nearer than when we first believed."

God does not want us to live in fear, but we need to be aware
of these things and the time in which we're living, and make
sure our hearts are in right relationship with Him. The question
for each of us is, *"Am I ready for His coming?"*

If your heart is right with Him, then there is no need to fear,
for your future is secure with God in Christ, regardless of what
is happening in the world around you.

However, if you've never committed your heart and life to
Christ, or if you have strayed away from your relationship with
Him, then the first and most important thing is laid out for us in
Acts 3:19 (NKJV) which tells us:

"Repent therefore and be converted, that your sins may be blotted out, so that times of refreshing may come from the presence of the Lord."

The truth is if we as individuals and as a nation will repent and turn our hearts back to God, He will again forgive and bless, heal our lives, and our nation. He forgives and refreshes those who seek Him.

Part of our preparation for Christ's return is to do all we can to share the good news of Christ's love with people who come into our lives, sharing what God has done for us, and His love for them. Whenever we pray for someone to come to know Christ and share with them even in the smallest way about God's goodness, we are partners with God to bring them to Him.

We also prepare ourselves for His coming by faithfully running the race that is set before us, staying close with Christ through prayer and time spent with Him reading His Word. We need to focus on the things of eternal value and stay occupied with the things that He values. Even though the trials you or I may be facing today are overwhelming, there is a Scripture from Psalm 61 that lifts me and reminds me to go to my Rock, verses 1 and 2 (NKJV):

"Hear my cry, O God; attend to my prayer. From the end of the earth I will cry to You, when my heart is overwhelmed; lead me to the rock that is higher than I."

You have Someone greater than your trials today and the challenges of tomorrow. You have God Himself, your Rock upon Whom you can rest secure, and His promises which cannot fail. He is faithful to watch over His Word to perform it. He is so intentional about honoring His Word in one Scripture He declares that He honors His Word above His own Name. The Word also states in one verse that heaven and earth shall pass away but His Word will remain forever.

The last part of our preparation in anticipation of His coming is to stand firm against the schemes of our enemy, satan. As previously mentioned, we are to put on the whole armor of God and after we've done all, to stand. In the book of James we're told that if we resist the devil he will flee from us. If you are in Christ, you are God's child and you have no need to fear satan. But be aware of his tactics and don't buy into his lies that cause you to live in fear by focusing on the things in the world, or living for yourself, or fearing to speak out for what is right and true. Remember, if you are God's child you have authority in Jesus to stand against the lies of the evil one, and in Jesus' Name as you resist him, he has to flee.

We are told in James 5:8 (NIV): *"You, too, be patient and stand firm, because the Lord's coming is near."* You can be sure that when Jesus does return, He will be bringing His rewards with Him, overflowing to those who have loved and served Him faithfully.

We haven't yet begun to experience the glory that awaits those whose hearts belong to Him. II Corinthians 2:9 (NKJV) promises:

"...Eye has not seen, nor ear heard, nor have entered into the heart of man the things which God has prepared for those who love Him."

"He who testifies to these things says, 'Surely I am coming quickly.' Amen. Even so, come, Lord Jesus!" Revelation 22:20 (NKJV)

Appendix

SCRIPTURES ON THE RETURN OF CHRIST

The Timing of His Return

Matthew 24:27, Matthew 24:36-42, Luke 12:40,
I Thessalonians 5:2, Revelation 3:3, Revelation 16:15.

The Nearness of His Return

Philippians 4:4,5, Hebrews 10:37, James 5:8, Revelation 3:11,
Revelation 22:7, Revelation 22:20.

Preparing for His Return

Matthew 24:44, Luke 19:13, I Corinthians 1:7-9,
I Thessalonians 5:23,24, I Timothy 6:11-14, Titus 2:11-13,
I John 2:28

Rewards for Believers When He Returns

Luke 12:37-38, John 14:3, Philippians 3:20,21,
Colossians 3:4, I Thessalonians 3:12,13

About the Author

Ruth Knoblock is a leader of women's Bible studies and prayer groups. She presents workshops on Prayer, and Friendship with God, and is a guest speaker at retreats and other gatherings. She is a much sought-after mentor of women of all ages. Her passion is to see men and women embrace their true identity in Christ and become all God created them to be.

Ruth raised five children with her husband, Jim. She loves to travel, and has lived in nine different states, including California, New York, New Mexico, and Idaho, where she currently resides.

She revels in God's creation, and loves to be outdoors. In her youth, Ruth was pitcher on her softball team. A chapter in this book, describing the tale of her "roller derby award," demonstrates her zest for life and active sense of humor.

Blessed with a beautiful singing voice, she loves music, especially the song, *You Raise Me Up,* because, she says, "It describes my whole life's experience."

One of Ruth's favorite things on a cold winter's day is to curl up with a good book, a warm comforter, and a hot vanilla latté.

Ruth can be contacted by email:
ruthieknoblock@yahoo.com

These blank pages are here for you to record your own

study notes and thoughts.

www.ingramcontent.com/pod-product-compliance
Lightning Source LLC
Chambersburg PA
CBHW031850090426
42741CB00005B/429